Practical Thought Models for Men

Use mental techniques of the world's greatest leaders to make better decisions, conquer any obstacle, build self-confidence and make lasting progress in life and work

John Adams

© **Copyright 2019 - All rights reserved.**

The content contained within this book may not be reproduced, duplicated or transmitted without direct written permission from the author or the publisher.

Under no circumstances will any blame or legal responsibility be held against the publisher, or author, for any damages, reparation, or monetary loss due to the information contained within this book. Either directly or indirectly.

Legal Notice:

This book is copyright protected. This book is only for personal use. You cannot amend, distribute, sell, use, quote or paraphrase any part, or the content within this book, without the consent of the author or publisher.

Disclaimer Notice:

Please note the information contained within this document is for educational and entertainment purposes only. All effort has been executed to present accurate, up to date, and reliable, complete information. No warranties of any kind are declared or implied. Readers acknowledge that the author is not engaging in the rendering of legal, financial, medical or professional advice. The content within this book has been derived from various sources. Please consult a licensed professional before attempting any techniques outlined in this book.

By reading this document, the reader agrees that under no circumstances is the author responsible for any losses, direct or indirect, which are incurred as a result of the use of information contained within this document, including, but not limited to, — errors, omissions, or inaccuracies.

Hello,

As an independent author,
   and one-man operation
   - my marketing budget is next to zero.

As such, the only way
   I can get my books in-front of valued customers
   is with reviews.

Unfortunately, I'm competing against authors and
   giant publishing companies
   with multi-million-dollar marketing teams.

These behemoths can afford
   to give away hundreds of free books
   to boost their ranking and success.

Which as much as I'd love to –
   I simply can't afford to do.

That's why your honest review
   will not only be invaluable to me,
     but also to other readers on Amazon.

Happy reading,

John Adams

Table of Contents

Introduction	**9**
Chapter 1: I Don't Use Models, Or Do I?	**17**
Mental Models Explained	18
Mental Models: The Good	21
Mental Models: The Bad	23
Mental Models: A Better Approach	25
Chapter 2: I Know It Better... Or Not?	**35**
Selective Perception	35
Perception and Decision-Making	38
Expanding Your Perception	41
Confirmation Bias	44
Examples of Confirmation Bias	44
Avoiding Confirmation Bias	47
Framing	49
Examples of Framing in Real Life	51
How to Use Framing to Your Advantage	53
Chapter 3: Let's Do It Like This... Or Wait... Maybe...	**61**
Common Mistakes in Decision-Making	63
Elon Musk: An Embodiment of First-Principle Thinking	69
Ray Dalio: Decision Making with Second-Order Thinking	74
Jeff Bezos: Thinking on Your Feet	79
More Mental Models for Making Better Decisions	84
Bottom Line	90
Chapter 4: This Can Be Done Faster...	**93**

Thing You Do That Prevents Productivity	94
Mental Models for Optimizing Productivity	99
Mental Models for System Thinking	117
Chapter 5: Getting Want You Want... Like This	**131**
Common Persuasion Mistakes	131
The Psychology of Persuasion	135
The Power of "Because": The Mental Model of Reason Respecting	147
Warren Buffett: A Few Practical Lessons in Persuasion	150
Conclusion	**155**
Other Books by John Adams	**161**
References	**163**

Introduction

It feels great to set definite goals, work towards them, and achieve them. Although this may not happen 100% of the time, it is still a great morale booster. On the flip side, it is frustrating to have most of your best efforts truncated because of poor decisions, wrong choices, and error in judgment. The experience of continuous failure can be demoralizing and can lead to throwing in the towel. This unpleasant experience seems to be the lot of the average modern man (and woman too!) who are continually faced with several challenges, which they must overcome or risk feeling insignificant.

As a man, your challenges may appear peculiar to you depending on what you are trying to accomplish, your priorities in life, and what is most important to you, but the truth is that you are in the same boat with more people than you realize. You may be trying to:

- Overcome procrastination and get things done at the right time.

- Manage your anger which tends to be destroying a lot of your personal and professional relationships.

- Improve your communication that you've found to be ineffective and lead to frequent misunderstandings and unsaid intentions.

- Cope with the stress of a demanding job or career.

- Raise your teenagers in the best way possible without losing your mind.

- Manage your lean finances – a feat for which many people seem to lack the very fundamentals.

- Improve your time management by strictly keeping family and work completely separate or figuring out how best to share your time between your team and your primary schedule.

- Work on improving your failing self-confidence, poor self-esteem, and a general poor self-image.

- Overcoming lust and pornography – two factors that are negatively affecting your relationship with the opposite sex.

- Improve your failing marriage or struggling to fix intimacy issues.

- Overcome addiction to alcohol or other unhealthy substances.

- Reduce weight and stay true to a diet program.

- Overcome pride that can lead to living in denial or refusing to admit that you even have issues with these challenges to begin with.

Whatever your particular situation is, you are not alone. Every single adult, regardless of race, belief, gender, financial status, and so on, has one or more challenging situation that they are working to overcome. The difference is that while successful people have internalized certain principles that help them learn faster, think better, and decide smarter, the majority of the other "struggling" people are groping in the darkness of erroneous thinking patterns.

It doesn't matter how well-intentioned you are, if you live your life based on a false premise or based on faulty thinking, your results will most likely be short of what you truly desire. This brings to mind the picture of a bird smashing into a glass window in the hope of getting to the vegetation reflected on the glass or in the hope of flying through it as it reflects the sky. Although the bird can see the glass, its limited or faulty thinking pattern (its mental model) does not permit it to see the error in its interpretation of reality. Forcefully, it hits the glass and dies on the spot or gets stunned and gradually recovers to try again using the same pattern of thinking!

Repeating the same thing can only guarantee one outcome: the same result! This can be tiring and frustrating (not for the birds; I'm talking about us humans!) It is the frustration that comes from repeated failure that often leads to some ridiculous conclusions about cause and effect. The worst kind of thinking would be to attribute your repeated failures to some spiritual forces which are meddling in your personal affairs. As much as that could be a plausible argument, your best bet to making failure a less-occurring feature in your life is to change your thought patterns.

We are all on a journey of seeking the truth (about different aspects of our lives), problem solving, and decision making. Every single day, and for more times than we care to note, we make decisions. It seems our lives are a string of decisions and choices. This means that the more wrong choices we make, the unhappier our lives will be. And the righter choices or decisions we make, the happier and more fulfilled our lives will be. Therefore, we must devote our time to learning methods that can help us make sense of our daily challenging situations, help us generate better ideas, and also help us in our decision-making process. In other words, we must give our undivided attention to developing ways that can help us approach challenging situations in more innovative and novel ways. This can only be possible if we are willing to be malleable and give up the thinking patterns that are no longer useful to us, irrespective of how dear they are to us.

You do not need to have a desire to be the next Albert Einstein or Jeff Bezos for you to find this book useful. As a matter of fact, this book was primarily written for those who simply want to make sense of their day-to-day challenges and live a more fulfilled life, even if that means simplifying their decision-making process. Whether you are a parent seeking better ways to handle the upbringing of your children, a team leader at work trying to cope with the stress of leadership, a budding business owner who is in search of better ways to make more profit, or an employee who just wants to improve his career, this book will guide you on how to make quality decisions to improve your quality of thinking. When you make more good decisions than you make bad ones, you improve your chances of getting promoted at work, attracting opportunities in business, gaining more respect from family, friends, and colleagues, and becoming a better person on the whole.

The concepts and ideas that are shared in this book are capable of challenging your assumptions and tightly held beliefs about life. But beyond challenging your suppositions, beliefs, and specific ways of thinking, this book will feed your mind and help you to become wiser and more discerning of situations. The goal of this book is to help men the world over live a more fulfilled and meaningful life by sharing thought-provoking mental models that will nudge them towards making fewer wrong choices.

Although this book, Mental Model for Men, tends to be gender-biased, women too can benefit immensely from it because the mental models work based on principles that are not gender-based. Society tends to put the responsibility for living successful lives more on the shoulders of men. We have come to accept that the man should fend for his family (wife and children) and that is not a light burden. The pressure from the home front and that from work can make the average man cringe in pain. But with the right mental model, he can leverage time-tested principles and succeed faster than his peers.

This book will present several short stories of successful men in many areas of life, great leaders, and captains of industry, all of whom have had cause to face challenges similar to the ones you are facing today and overcame. Nevertheless, the focus of this book is not the successful people; instead, the focus is on the methods that brought about their success. Often, it can be annoying to read about business moguls and their huge financial empires when you can barely stop yourself from losing money on your tiny investments. I do not intend to wow you with the impressive achievements of famous people. No. Those are not the types of stories I intend to share with you. To begin with, you may not even be interested in becoming a captain of any industry or a leader in your company. My goal for presenting you with some of these inspiring stories is to demonstrate the practicability of these mental models in everyday life.

This book shall take you through some of your biases and prejudices that are preventing you from objectively considering your situations and the many challenging issues that confront your almost daily. We shall take a somewhat rollercoaster ride across several mental models to help you see your live events from different perspectives because the more you can master multiple mental models, the more options and approaches you can apply to different situations in your life.

But beyond different mental models, this book will help you to understand how to apply these models in your life. I have downplayed the theories and academic works relating to mental models and presented only the facts and details you need to make high-quality decisions, simply your decision-making process, and reduce your biases. Therefore, expect to get information that can:

- Help you make faster decisions.

- Work more efficiently as you apply simple but effective principles.

- Help you gain new insights on how to overcome the challenges that are making you feel stuck in your professional and personal life.

As much as I would like for you to quickly devour the contents of this book, I encourage you to take your time to comprehend the information contained in this book. Keep in mind that, as with many other things in life, consistent practice is what leads to mastery. You're not going to magically transform your thought processes or thinking pattern by merely reading this book or any other for that matter! A lot of effort is required on your part – the practical application of what you have learned.

I urge you to begin with baby steps. Apply these mental models consistently and see how they positively impact one simple area of your life where you do not have serious challenges. Little by little, you will gain more confidence to take on more challenging areas of your life. In all likelihood, the positive changes you seek will not happen overnight, but it will definitely happen if you remain consistent.

Here is to a happy and more fulfilled you as you learn and apply the mental models of the ultra-successful of our world.

Chapter 1: I Don't Use Models, Or Do I?

Picture in your mind's eye for a minute, a drunk frantically looking for his house keys at night, but he is only searching under the streetlight because his hazed mind tells him that's where the light is. He can only see where there is light, so he doesn't bother to look for his keys where there is no light. Perhaps, if he were sober, he could have figured out that his keys could be anywhere whether there was light or not.

Analogies are hardly perfect, but the above scenario captures the essence of mental models. You can only figure out things to the extent your mental model permits. If you have a mental model of the drunk, your search for success, more money, efficiency, time management, love, and so on, will be limited to where there is light. You will not bother to look where the beam of the streetlight can't reach because your model doesn't support it. Your life can only be as great as your mental models.

To assess whether your mental models are good and useful, you should evaluate the results you have in every aspect of your life. For many people, this assessment has driven them to search for better ways to approach their life's challenges. And that search has resulted in reading this book. They understand that to effectively change their approach, there is a need to adjust their internal picture of how the world works.

But what if you don't use a mental model? Or do we all use one? Well, to answer that, let's first see what mental models are.

Mental Models Explained

According to the Business Dictionary website, mental models are "Beliefs, ideas, images, and verbal descriptions that we consciously or unconsciously form from our experiences and which (when formed) guide our thoughts and actions within narrow channels" (BusinessDictionary.com, n.d.). In simple English, a mental model is a mental representation of your world's view. It is your perception of what reality is (and isn't) and it plays a major role in how you behave and respond to the situations you encounter daily.

When you picture a challenging situation your mind predicts or figures out an outcome using a set of ideas and assumptions you have built over time, that is your mental model at work. We all use mental models in our daily lives. It doesn't matter whether you are aware of it or not; it certainly doesn't matter if you took the time to build or formulate one for yourself or not. The fact is that all of us use mental models, and by the way, that's a good thing! Your thought processes about how something works is a mental model for that thing. Your conception of a thing, your expected results and consequences of specific actions, your interpretation of events, and your problem-solving approach are all as a reflection of your mental model.

Here's a simplified example of how mental models work. Let us assume that you are playing a game with a young child of about 7 years old using a scale model of the house you currently live in. The model house is complete with furnishing. You hide a miniature book in the closet of the model house while the child carefully observes the location of the hidden book. Now you ask the child to locate the real book in the real house. Guess where he or she will look first? In the closet! A younger child of 2 or 3 years old may look in several locations before going to the closet. But at 7, the child is wise enough to analogize the house in his head. That is how we all have the world in our heads – as little maps that help use "locate" (figure out) solutions.

In general, we tend to unconsciously develop several mental models from when we were little toddlers. Events that shape our world when we were children tend to shape our perspective for a lifetime unless of course, we deliberately make the effort to change such mental models. For example, if a child grows up in a dysfunctional family where he is exposed to incessant fights, violence, and physical abuse (either on him or between his parents), it wouldn't be surprising for such a child to grow up into thinking and behaving in ways that can result in a series of dysfunctional relationships in his adult years. This is because, over time, he has developed an unhealthy mental model about relationships.

Equally, a boy that grows up in a home where both parents work outside the home tends to build a mental model where both parents need to work to take care of the family. He will likely grow up to prefer women who work outside the home. His choice of a life partner is most likely to be influenced by the mental model he developed while growing up.

You may not realize it, but almost every decisive choice you make and important action you take in your life passed through the filter of the models you carry around in your head. Just like the 7-year-old who searched first in the closet, your choices and actions, even though they may appear random to you, are dictated by your mental models. Perhaps you need to pause and ask yourself why your default behavior in certain situations is not the same as the next person's default behavior. The answer lies in the behavior of the 7-year-old after observing the model house! Looking first in the closet can be described as a default behavior. When you have observed different models life has exposed you to for a long time, your default behavior will result from such mental models.

So, if your life's results are not too satisfactory or you have been struggling for a while to break free from a streak of failure and struggles, you need to start taking a look at other models that have worked for other people.

Mental Models: The Good

On one hand, mental models create a sense of internal stability in the individual. This is particularly useful if you consider that the world we live in is constantly changing. I mean, imagine what it will look like if you were to wake up each morning and begin to learn afresh how to approach every single thing in your life all over again (like a 2-year-old kid searching for the hidden book!) There is a need for a certain level of stability to prevent you from being swept by every wind of change. This makes it possible for you to approach challenging situations with time-tested ideologies that worked over and again without wasting time, energy, and resources. If you are losing money or missing out on great opportunities in life, it is an indication that you are working with mental models that are no longer serving you. This means you need to unlearn what you knew previously and learn a new set of mental models.

Periodically, organizations analyze the mental models of their customers (using surveys) to find out what their customers' biases and preferences are and then tailor their products and services towards those biases. Does that not make you want to have a second thought about how important mental models are? I mean, think about it for a minute. Why would multinational corporations go through all the trouble of analyzing mental models of their customers? Here are a few reasons they do that:

- To understand the minds of their customers.

- To gather real-world perspectives about their services.

- To use the information they gathered to improve their customers' experience.

- To guide them to think strategically about the solutions for their customers' problems.

- To expose areas where they are making wrong assumptions about customer's needs.

- To recognize new opportunities.

- To recognize faults in current solutions and seek ways to fix them.

All these translate into more profits, more opportunities, and more customer satisfaction. But we are not talking about companies or customers; our focus is on you – the struggling individual who wants to seize more of his opportunities, make more money, increase his chances of getting promoted, minimize his chances of failure in his investments, managing his time more effectively, get his family life in order, or create more happiness in his life. These can only be achieved by a shift in your thinking processes because your actions result from your thoughts. So, if we can dig down to the faulty thought processes and install a new set of mental models that work, your actions and subsequent results will reflect the new change you seek.

Mental Models: The Bad

On the other hand, there are some huge drawbacks to mental models. If these drawbacks are not recognized, it can lead the individual into very myopic and incorrect worldviews. As you may have deduced by now, maps are not 100% the same as the real world. What you have in your head as mental models are mere maps; they do not contain every single detail of the real world, nor should they. Overdependence on an analogy, as you know, is like staking your hard-earned money on a leaky bucket; one moment it is full; the next, it is completely empty!

We have to be careful not to be fixated on one mental model. There is no one mental model that is suitable for all situations. As a matter of fact, a mental model that worked for one situation may fail when applied to another situation because, as earlier stated, we live in a constantly changing world. Becoming set in your mental model and refusing to change even when there is glaring evidence that suggests the need for a different approach can lead to unnecessary suffering, loss of time and energy.

This is why many men – good men, I must add – who are working hard on their dreams never seem to achieve those dreams. They put in a lot of effort, but the rewards in terms of money, time, freedom, love, ease, promotion, building teams and systems, and so on, seem to constantly elude them. Reaching your desired goals is not just about being good, nor is it about having noble intentions. It is one thing to want to be a great father, for example, but if your mental model about family and relationship is faulty, then your best intentions will always meet a Waterloo. To correct this, there is a need to properly scrutinize your thought processes with a view to finding out where the error in thinking lies. It is like taking apart the various sections of a faulty computer program to isolate which section is encoded wrongly and causing the error in the entire program – a process known as debugging.

But, just as it happens in effective debugging, you need to think things through before delving into the program code and changing things. Usually, when you shift commands around in the code, that section of the program may work well because you have isolated and fixed the local issue. But another problem will soon arise that will make you start the debugging process all over again. However, when you take the time to think about how the bug (fault or problem) began, you will most likely discover how to improve the entire program design and put a stop to more bugs.

This book is designed to offer you debugging options that will help you dig deep into your ideologies and fish out exactly what has been preventing you from hitting your target in spite of your best intentions. But beyond isolating bugs and faults in thinking and beyond looking at your life's program code line after line to trace where the bugs could be, we shall see how to consider the entire program for each aspect of your life and see what models work best for them. We shall go into various mental models that can be very useful, but first, you need to understand that, like many other things in life, mental models can be fallible.

Mental Models: A Better Approach

Change is constant! Have I said that enough times yet? Well, there is a reason I keep repeating that. Humans tend to stick to something if it works a few times. We are quick to declare, "I have discovered the truth! This is my secret formula for success!" We then go ahead to overuse that one formula or approach for every problem we face. But the fact that something worked for a particular situation doesn't automatically mean it will work for every situation. We must keep in mind that what we regard as truth is subjective and can become obsolete with time.

Consider, as an example, the approach of Niels Bohr, one of the pioneers of quantum physics, when he was trying to understand the dual nature of matter. (Don't worry; I'm not going to bore you with any physics jargon!) For nearly two decades, Bohr tried to understand why photons show up as waves in an experiment, yet the same photons show up as particles if the experiment is set up another way. It simply doesn't make any sense, nor does it agree with any of the laws of our physical universe known to man at that time. But the real problem Bohr had was in his mental model. He was using an outmoded model to figure out a solution for a phenomenon that is on a higher level of understanding. Niels Bohr finally came to understand that quantum physics was on a higher level of truth than the Newtonian physics the world was used to at that time (Scientific Thought: In Context, 2009).

There were several truths that were displaced by higher truths, not because the lower truths were false, but because they were no longer applicable given the current circumstances. Higher truths, must out of necessity, build on lower truths. For example, Newtonian physics displaced Aristotelian worldview by building on what was previously true in the Aristotelian era. Einstein's physics displaced the lower truths presented by Newtonian physics, and quantum physics displaced some of the lower truths in Einstein's physics. None of these previously held ideologies were wrong; they only presented solutions based on the level of understanding they were exposed to at that time.

Here's how all this apply to you. When situations change, it will be almost impossible to approach the new change with lower truths or understanding. In other words, having a static mental model is simply a precursor for failure. Remember the analogy in the introduction of the bird flying into the glass window? That's exactly what it looks like when you keep approaching situations with lower truths or outmoded mental models. They may have worked for some situations in the past, but in the light of current events, they are no longer useful. The approach that worked for the successful man in the Stone Age must be discarded in the Iron Age if man must experience any semblance of success. Equally, the mental model of the Iron Age must give way in the Industrial Age, if man must make significant progress. You must be open and willing to embrace change that displaces your previously held mental models if you must keep up with changing times and situations.

Forget Perfection, Focus on Applicability

I strongly suggest that you approach the use of mental models from an angle that considers how useful they are in the daily application instead of how perfect the models are. As the famous British statistician, George Box, puts it, "All models are approximations. Essentially, all models are wrong, but some are useful. However, the approximate nature of the model must always be borne in mind" (Box, 1987, p. 424).

In other words, give up the search for one particular "secret" to success! There is no such thing as one mental model that is perfect for all situations. What you should concern yourself with is thinking about the utility of a model rather than its accuracy in all situations. The more a mental model can help you to figure out how to tackle everyday challenges, the better and more useful it is.

However, given the fact that no one mental model is suitable for every situation, your best bet is to be open to developing a collection of mental models that you can use collectively to approach problems and decision making. This makes good sense because the more mental models you can access, the better your chances of making better decisions or fewer wrong decisions. Someone with only a handful of mental models is limited to think from the few models he has. He can't see beyond his limited models; therefore, his choices and subsequent outcomes are limited.

Imagine for a minute that you are a carpenter with only a hammer and a bunch of nails in your tool belt. Hammering nails and banging things into place is about all the options you have. But that is pretty limiting to accomplish any meaning task. This brings to mind the saying, "To the man with only a hammer, every problem looks like a nail!" Now imagine what it would be like to have your tool belt packed and ready with screws, utility knife, hammer, pliers, pencil, nail sets, electrical tape, and a screwdriver. That gives you a whole lot of options and choices. You can fix and invent several things because your creative juices have been given a boost!

That is exactly how having access to several useful mental models work. The more mental models you can apply to different areas of your life, the more you call forth your ingenuity to handle everyday situations.

Here's an example that illustrates how to combine different mental models for boosting creativity in your life. I'll use three different mental models for a fictitious character called Sam.

Lately, Sam has been worried about his productivity level which seems to be consistently going down in recent times. He is a struggling blogger who is trying to break even. He battles with procrastination and a general lack of time management. He feels overwhelmed at the number of things he has to do every day just to stay afloat and not be drowned by his family responsibilities and job demands. He spends more time on his phone chatting with friends because that seems to be the only time he has some sense of happiness, but that habit robs him of his time. Although he is reluctant about giving it up, he realizes that he needs to go social media cold turkey if he must increase his productivity both at home and at work.

Sam stumbles on a great book that explains the use of different mental models. He identified three mental models that can help him with his current challenge, namely; the Ivy Lee method, the 2-minute rule, and the Seinfeld strategy. He understands that none of these models are perfect on their own, but he found a way to combine them to help him get over his procrastination and addiction to social media.

First, Sam began deliberately planning his day from the previous night by creating a to-do list of the most important things he would like to achieve the next day. But he didn't just write out one long list; he went over his list pruning it down to only six items and prioritizing them according to their order of importance and urgency. By doing this, he was utilizing the Ivy Lee method.

Next, he committed to taking action immediately. He began to consider the time it took to accomplish certain tasks and discovered a whole lot of tasks could be accomplished in two minutes or less as suggested by the 2-minute rule. So, Sam began getting many of his tasks done more effectively. Tasks like sending a quick email, cleaning up clutter, taking out the garbage, and so on were handled immediately. Sometimes, he still had the urge to put some things off, especially when they take more than two minutes to accomplish, but he took that as his cue to work on them immediately. When he identified tasks that took more than two minutes to accomplish, Sam simply started the process of accomplishing them in two minutes or less. So, when he has a big task like writing a blog, he started with just a sentence but later finds he has written for more than an hour! When he was feeling lazy about reading a whole book, he simply read a couple of paragraphs and before he knows it, he was neck-deep in the book.

Keeping this habit up was a bit of a challenge. But thanks to the Seinfeld strategy, Sam was able to remain consistent about his new habit. He made a commitment to spend only one hour a day on social media, write for two hours a day, and then place a checkmark on his calendar to indicate that he has successfully accomplished his goals for the day. Sam wasn't too focused on his results as he was concerned about sticking to his commitment and seeing the unbroken chain of marks on his calendar. Before long, Sam's productivity skyrocketed, and he was able to manage his time better. His struggle with procrastination is now a thing of the past and he is able to take action right away on things that are important to him.

But Sam's success isn't so much of a surprise because he was using the mental models of successful people. Take the Seinfeld strategy for example. The strategy was named after Jerry Seinfeld whose remarkable consistency led to incredible successes. In 1998, he became the highest annual earner ever for a TV actor, and he holds the Guinness World Record for that (Guinness World Record, 1999). Little wonder those who

31

use this mental model like artist, CEOs, athlete, and so on (including Sam in our example) are likely to be more productive than their peers.

Let me bring this chapter to a close a brief story. This time it is a true story of one of the billionaires of our time – Charles "Charlie" Thomas Munger, the American investor, businessman, and philanthropist.

Many people think that attaining success is all about setting goals, having a vision, and working hard to achieve those goals. However, things usually go wrong no matter how great our visions are and how lofty our goals may be. When things do go wrong, we are quick to blame ourselves for not staying through to our visions and goals.

Charlie Munger trained as a lawyer at Harvard and a meteorologist in the days of World War II. He later committed to learning several disciplines like history, economics, biology, physics, psychology, and a few others. This gave him an edge in exploring several great mental models that helped him overcome complex problems.

One of his successful approaches to accomplishing great feats was being both optimistic and pessimistic at the same time. This may come as counterproductive to the mental model of being optimistic at all times and in all situations, but Munger's mental model worked and his results are very glaring (he is a billionaire for God's sake!)

Munger thought through what could possibly go wrong with his projects and investments. He looked at a situation backwards, upside down, and inside out to figure out every possible thing that can go wrong. This is known as reverse thinking. In his words, "What happens if all our plans go wrong? Where don't we want to go, and how do you get there? Instead of looking for success, make a list of how to fail instead; through sloth, envy, resentment, self-pity, entitlement, all the mental habits of self-defeat. Avoid these qualities and you will succeed. Tell me where I'm going to die so I don't go there" (Munger, 2005).

This approach helped Munger to stay away from solutions that only looked good temporary and only worked with solutions that are long lasting. The approach helped him to avoid pitfalls and roadblocks; and in the event that something goes wrong, Munger was more disposed to handling it. In essence, Muller combined both goal setting and invert thinking to achieve success.

While positive thinking can lead to success, envisioning obstacles and building your life's plan to avoid those obstacles can bring lasting success devoid of a constant need to debug and figure out what is wrong with your plan.

Munger's mental model that led to his success story can be

summarized in one simple sentence: the most effective way to avert trouble is to steer clear of it altogether by discovering what works and what doesn't.

Chapter 2: I Know It Better... Or Not?

You can only see what you want to see. If you think something is irrelevant your mind will filter it out and make only relevant things dominant in your perception. Your mind helps you to pick out only things you believe to be true or supports your belief. This is how your reality and life experience is shaped. Your mind helps you do all this to keep you sane! And I'll show you in a bit how all these happen. The downside to keeping you sane is that you tend to think in stereotypes or allow default thinking to run your decisions. In other words, you become biased to certain beliefs. This causes you to think that you know better unless you become deliberate and start forcing your brain to actually think! In this chapter, we shall take a close look at some of the mental biases that can greatly influence our decision-making process and ultimately our behaviors.

Selective Perception

If you were to respond to the entire stimulus coming at you every single second, you would be worse than insane! In fact, it is practically impossible to think, feel, and see everything in your reality at the same time. This is why you can only see what you want to see. Here's an interesting piece of science fact: the human brain can only process only about 50 bits of information per second out of the 11 million bits sent to it every single second (Encyclopedia Britannica, n.d.).

If you find it difficult to accept this, I invite you to try this simple exercise. Get a pen and a piece of paper and begin to write down all the things that you can see, feel, taste, smell, and hear right now. After writing for about 5 minutes, you'll discover that you are ignoring to write down some stimulus. Why is that so? It's simple: you simply cannot keep up with the entire stimulus coming at you at the same time.

What is Selective Perception?

Your brain helps you to focus only on things that you've consciously or subconsciously instructed it to focus on through a process known as selective perception. Selective perception is the process where your brain analyzes, categorizes, and selects stimuli from your environment that resonates with your belief or focus and discards or blocks out stimuli that are not in agreement with your belief or focus.

The Problem with Selective Perception?

Getting us to focus on the task at hand is a good thing and helps us to concentrate. But as noble as selective perception may be, it has an inherent drawback. We are not always good at telling our brains what is relevant and what is not. And I am not just referring to minor errors in perception. For example, In *How Doctors Think*, Jerome Groopman, M.D. notes that 60% of trained radiologist failed to notice a missing collarbone in someone's chest x-ray due to an analysis that influenced their perception (Groopman, 2007, p. 179).

The implication of this is that even in serious situations or when faced with major life-altering decisions, you could be missing out important pieces of information because of how your mind has been conditioned by your beliefs.

Your ability to focus on one thing means other things are automatically out of focus. Anyone who knows how to use a camera will tell you that! This is why a smoker can read an entire magazine and even make some purchases from the adverts in the magazine but completely fail to notice all the warnings against smoking in the same magazine. His selective perception blocks out those warnings because they don't agree with his set of beliefs.

Selective perception is the reason we tend to overestimate our capacity to make rational decisions and criticize others for being partial. But if you take the time to really scrutinize your decisions, you will discover that it is almost impossible to escape this naturally occurring bias. For example, in a soccer match, we can quickly point out acts of partiality when the referee appears to be deliberately favoring a team we don't support. However, we conveniently ignore it when the same referee awards the team we support an unjustified penalty.

If you take a little time to think about it, sexism, racism, and other types of discrimination stem from selective perception. Your prejudice can stop you from accepting useful information from a certain group of people because they don't fit into the category you deem useful or good. This is exactly why someone from a particular religion or political party can easily dismiss information from other groups because his filter doesn't favor their views. I am not suggesting that you should accept every data (stimuli from all sources) without scrutinizing it. However, when you begin to eliminate "inconvenient data," you are leaning more toward auto-pilot behavior instead of deliberate or conscious behavior.

Perception and Decision-Making

Question: How do we make decisions that are not based on limited perception?

Short answer: You don't!

Long answer: Your perceptions will always be limited to some extent. The best you can do is to expand your perception to include a wider range of information that you'll ordinarily be closed off to. We'll see how to do just that in the next section. Attempting to critically analyze a problem or situation from all possible angles can lead to analysis paralysis – a situation where no forward movement in terms of decision or cause of action is reached. For now, let us see how you can use the rational decision-making model to sidestep negative and narrow perceptions.

The Rational Decision-Making Model

I do not intend to go into any lengthy lecture about the theories of this mental model. I'll simply explain what it is and the steps involved in using it.

The rational decision-making model is a process involving a series of steps geared towards problem-solving beginning at defining the problem through selecting the best alternative given the available information. This model helps you look beyond your set of limiting beliefs to make logically sound decisions.

Below are the steps.

1. **Define the problem**: This involves stating exactly what the problem is and its cause (not the symptom). For example, you want to buy a bigger house because your family has outgrown the current one. The problem is not buying a new house; that is a symptom or an alternative solution. The real problem is inadequate space. Properly identifying the cause of the problem can help you think about your current state and the

desired state in a proper light. In our example, defining space as the cause of the problem can lead to comparing alternatives such as buying a new house, expanding the current house, or getting rid of unnecessary stuff to free up space.

2. **Identify the decision criteria:** The next step is to consider the available criteria. Using our example above, the criteria could be time and cost. Ask exactly when you will need the extra space, how long will each alternative take, and when would it become very crucial to solve that space problem. Consider how much each alternative will cost and how much money you have at hand or have access to.

3. **Assign weights to the criteria:** Next, weigh your options. You can compare your options to one another (relative comparison) to pick which one stands out as more important or use an absolute comparison method where you consider each alternative on its merit.

4. **List out alternatives:** Think up as many alternatives as possible that can solve the problem. It doesn't matter if an alternative appears good or bad; simply list them and think about them in the next step. Again, from our example, your alternatives to solving the space problem could be discarding unnecessary stuff, placing some rarely used possessions in storage, building additional

rooms, buying a new house, sending kids to a boarding house, and so on.

5. **Evaluate alternatives:** Use the criteria you have identified earlier in Step 2 to evaluate the alternatives you've listed to determine which option is more viable.

6. **Choose the optimal alternative:** From your evaluation, determine the best alternative and use that in making your decision.

This is just one model. There are several models you can use to reach logically sound and rational decisions. However, whichever model you wish to use in making your decisions, always keep in mind that models are logical and well organized only as ideas. In the real world, nothing is ever that way!

Expanding Your Perception

Obviously, you cannot use the entire information available to you at the same time. Some of them must be filtered out. But how can you broaden your perception so that you leave out less information?

The first step is becoming aware that you are constantly filtering information, which this chapter has exposed you to. Being aware that there is a problem usually is the first step towards successfully tackling the problem.

Secondly, and very importantly, there must be a willingness to deliberately shift your paradigm. This may not be a walk in the park for many people; the process can be really difficult and requires a lot of practice. "Drop all your mental conditioning and biases" is easy advice to give, but difficult to put into practice. And by the way, I dare say that's bad advice! Mental conditionings play vital roles in keeping us sane and efficient. Rather than attempting to give up all of your mental conditioning and biases (which is impossible!), I'll strongly suggest the following ways to help you expand your perception as well as help you avoid narrowmindedness.

1. Isolate one belief and try to question it. Give your mind permission to allow authentic answers come to you. Remember that when you ask genuine questions, you are inviting your mind to seek that which is broader than your current perspective.

2. Look for alternatives to that idea or belief. When you flip your belief over, you give knowledge room to grow and expand beyond your current reality.

3. Ask yourself if what you are observing or perceiving is really true or just one way to look at it. Remember that everything is perception! There is no such thing as absolute truth. Take time to probe your mind by asking questions such as "Am I missing something here?" "Is this information complete as it is?" "How else can I

look at this?"

4. Learn how to withhold judgment or criticism until you gather enough facts. This is particularly useful during conversations with your spouse or a coworker. As I write this, I recall a story shared by Stephen Covey in his book, *7 Habits of Highly Effective People.* A man whose children were disturbing almost everyone in a subway did not bother one bit to control them. They were so loud and irksome, yet the man paid no attention to them. When asked to bring his children to order, he quietly responded, "Oh, you're right. I guess I should do something about it. We just came from the hospital where their mother died about an hour ago. I don't know what to think, and I guess they don't know how to handle it either" (Covey, 1989). That response changed everything! More information was brought to light and all judgments and criticisms gave way to empathy and compassion.

5. Ask clarifying and leading questions during conversations whether it is in a professional or social interaction. This will bring more information to light and help you get the right perspective. To be sure you are on the same page and seeing things from the same perspective as the person you are interacting with, give them feedback about your understanding. For example,

"So, if get what you are saying correctly, you mean…" and state your understanding. Doing this can significantly reduce conflicts that can arise due to selective perception. It is not necessary that you must agree with the other person. However, a clearer understanding of their position helps you to relate better with them with fewer chances of misunderstandings.

Confirmation Bias

Very closely linked to selective perception is another cognitive bias known as the confirmation bias. This bias keeps you focused on gathering the information that supports your beliefs and disregards anything to the contrary. Many of us are genuinely convinced that our beliefs are very logical, rational, and impartial because we have experienced them for several years. However, many of us do not realize that our so-called impartial, logical, and rational beliefs were reinforced by our selective attention to "evidence" that support our beliefs.

Examples of Confirmation Bias

A clear example of confirmation bias is when someone who believes in extrasensory perception thinks about his friend and almost immediately gets an email from that friend. It reinforces his belief that what he thinks about is what happens in his reality. However, he ignores the very many times he has thought about that friend and many other friends without any of them calling, texting, or emailing him.

Another example of confirmation bias is when people support their favorite candidate and actively seek out examples of their "good" deeds to portray him or her in a good light. They are also quick to point out the "evil" deeds of the opposing candidate to paint him or her in a bad light. Perhaps, this behavior is best described in the following words, "Democrats will endorse an extremely restrictive welfare proposal, usually associated with Republicans, if they think it has been proposed by the Democratic Party. Republicans will support a generous welfare policy if they think it comes from the Republican Party. Label the same proposal as coming from the other side, and you might as well ask people if they will favor a policy proposed by Osama bin Laden" (Travis and Aronson, 2007).

Apart from personal beliefs, confirmation bias can also affect decision making in the work we do. As Groopman (2007) pointed out, confirmation bias can lead to misdiagnosis of patients. A doctor can form an opinion or a hypothesis about what a patient's diseases and then seek evidence that confirms that hypothesis while consciously or unconsciously ignoring evidence to the contrary.

In 2015, the National Lipid Association's former president

pushed for the use of the drug statin among the elderly to help in the reduction of cardiovascular occurrence (Thot, 2015). He cited one randomized control trial (the PROSPER study) to buttress his point but he overlooked another published randomized control trial (CORONA) which reported that statin made no significant impact on the reduction of cardiovascular events (DuBrof, 2017).

I'll like to cite one more example of confirmation bias as it affects our work and this is a very dicey topic for a lot of people. In the US, some (not all) law enforcement agents use their "discretionary" powers to treat people of color "differently" in places like airport, especially persons of Middle Eastern descent and Muslims. There is a phenomenon that has come to be known as "driving while black" in the US. These are clear examples of confirmation bias in law enforcement, especially in the US. This stereotypical way of thinking about black drivers among police officers in the US is as a result of confirmation bias. The police use legitimate reasons like broken tail lights to stop these black drivers and then seek evidence to confirm their preconceived notions about blacks. However, it is important to note that not all police officers engage in this behavior or share this faulty belief.

Avoiding Confirmation Bias

It is a bit tricky to completely avoid falling into the trap of confirmation bias (or any bias for that matter) because we all have confirmation bias to some degree. However, it can be significantly reduced to lessen its impact on our day-to-day decisions. You will find the following suggestions helpful in avoiding confirmation bias.

1. **Don't be Afraid to Expand Your Mind:** Expanding your mind does not mean you will automatically be brainwashed by ideas you don't subscribe to. Permit yourself to temporarily suspend your bias against an idea and then become an impartial observer of the idea to see its merits and demerits. Don't just throw away an opinion because it doesn't fit into your current set of beliefs. Your ability to give other people the benefit of a doubt both in social and professional interactions will allow you to reach more rational conclusions and decisions.

2. **Be Open to Opposing Views:** As obvious as this may be, it really is difficult to accept. Have you wondered why people often argue vigorously and fight over opposing views? It is because of the difficulty in being open to embracing ideas that conflict with theirs. And that is partly because they really don't know much

about their tightly held ideologies. Someone who cannot explain his ideology is likely to be a die-hard fanatic of that ideology and can easily resort to blind arguments and fights instead of tactful explanation and presentation of their ideas. Part of being open to opposing views requires being humble enough to ask questions about your ideologies and how you came to accept them as true.

3. **Test Ideologies:** As much as it is advisable to welcome opposing ideas, you need to be wary of buying in wholesale on the ideologies that are sold to you. Don't just accept an ideology because you read it in a book or because someone famous proposed it. Exercise your mind – put opposing ideas to test; question them before accepting or rejecting them.

4. **You Know Some Things... But You Don't Know It All:** Your ego sells you the idea that you know it better. It's okay to think that way but you need to realize that you don't know everything and your way of reasoning (no matter how rational it appears to you) can still be fraught with a lot of biases and errors. Acknowledging this fact requires a lot of humility – a virtue that is not very common in today's world.

5. **Embrace Surprises:** When things happen that you least expected, don't dismiss them because they don't

tally with your belief. Instead, begin to take a closer look into them with a view to refining some of your beliefs that were unsettled by the surprise. This is how new the frontiers of knowledge are expanded.

Keep in mind that your ideology is the filter through which you sift your world. The narrower your ideologies are, the more close-minded you become, and the less you are able to think for yourself or expand your thinking beyond its current capacity. The impacts of your ideology are not just on the work you do – your profession – but also on your relationship with your close friends and family, and on the day-to-day decisions you make. One of Charlie Munger's popular quotes reads thus, "Another thing I think should be avoided is extremely intense ideology because it cabbages up one's mind… When you're young, it's easy to drift into loyalties and when you announce that you're a loyal member and you start shouting the orthodox ideology out, what you're doing is pounding it in, pounding it in, and you're gradually ruining your mind" (Munger, 2007).

Framing

What do you see when you look at a glass of water with the water level at the midpoint? Is the glass half-full or half-empty? The answer to that depends on how the information is presented to you. Usually, you think about what the pros or what you stand to gain versus the cons or what you stand to lose when faced with a decision. But how the gain versus loss is portrayed has a lot to do with what your final decision would be. Naturally, if you think you'll lose more by making a certain decision, you will settle for an option that cuts your loses. This is what framing does; it influences you to see how making a choice will reduce your chances of loses.

What is Framing?

Framing is one of the cognitive biases that influence decision making based on how information or facts are presented. It is an alternative way of presenting previous information that significantly modifies a person's perceptions, assumptions, and decision regarding the information.

Consider the following statements:

1. If you are consistent with your medication, you're less likely to have a cardiac arrest.

2. If you are not consistent with your medication, you're increasing your chances of having a cardiac arrest.

Even though both statements are mathematically equivalent, the way the statements were framed makes the second one appear more effective than the first. This happens almost daily in our lives. The essence of framing can be simply summarized as what you say is not as important as how you say it (or what you perceive is not as important as how you perceive it).

Examples of Framing in Real Life

Framing is used in different facets of our lives to nudge us towards certain choices. In advertising, framing can be used to influence our buying choices. Here's an example that many people fall for. You see an item offered for a limited time as "2 for $2" and you quickly bought it like many other people. However, the unit price of the item is $1 and it is written (usually) in small print. There was no special offer, but it was framed to give that perception.

Dental care products are advertised in such a way that shows healthy gums, sparkling white teeth, fresh breath, and how that can make consumers more attractive to potential partners. Framed in such light, the next time the consumers' think of buying dental care products, their minds race back to the advert and they become more open to buying that particular product. Also, advertisers usually avoid words like "overpriced" and "expensive" when showcasing high-end products. Instead, they emphasize words like "luxurious" and "plus." Even when they advertise low-priced products, they don't use words like "sturdy and cheap," instead they conveniently say things like, "dependable and affordable."

In economics, an investor is likely to put his money into a company that is said to have 75% probability of making a profit than in a company is said to have 25% probability of having losses. Technically, both statements are the same, but the way the information is framed influenced the obvious choice.

Politicians use framing all the time to make the opposition appear incompetent while emphasizing only on their positive developments to frame the minds of the citizens towards giving them more votes.

One last example I'll like to share is a folklore that is popular among psychologists. It is a fictitious letter from a girl to her parents, narrating a series of unfortunate events that happened to her in school (Bronner, 2012, p. 69). She told them of how she suffered a concussion when she jumped out her a window in her dormitory during a fire outbreak. She informed her parents she was being cared for by a young man who witnessed the event and called the fire department and ambulance. She also informed them that the young man was not well educated, a different race and religion, and has a sexually transmitted disease which she caught from him. She's already pregnant and in love with him, and they intend to get married before the pregnancy begins to show. Finally, she informs them that she just made up everything she wrote, but that her grades are really bad.

This example may appear a little too extreme, but it perfectly highlights the use framing to help her parents receive the same information in the right perspective. Certainly, having poor grades is a lot better than that entire catastrophic episode.

How to Use Framing to Your Advantage

Deliberately framing a problem or a challenging situation can give you the perspective you need to make the right decisions. Your ability to decide whether or not a problem is worth solving depends on how you frame the problem. Equally, your success in making the right decisions depends, to a large extent, on how well you are able to deliberately frame situations to spur you into action. Leaving your brain to perceive your situations using your default perception process may lead to faulty choices because of the tendency of our brains to rely heavily on the first few pieces of data it has access to when we are faced with a decision.

Consider a situation where your spouse complains about how you give her too little attention because you are too consumed by your job and it is beginning to take its toll on your family life. You can think of the situation in the following ways:

1. I have to choose between her and my job!

2. I have to learn how to manage my time more.

Looking at the situation from the first frame of mind is likely to put you on the defensive. Instead of nudging you towards finding an amicable and mutually benefiting solution, it will lead you down the path of thinking she is selfish, too demanding, and ungrateful for your effort to cater to the family's need. This is bound to lead you to make decisions and take actions that will cause more conflicts in your relationship.

But framing the situation from the second perspective is likely to make you open to finding a balance between your job and family life. This line of thinking can make you live a healthier, happier, and more meaningful life devoid of unnecessary conflicts in your relationship.

Retraining Your Thinking

Considering how powerful the influence of framing can have on our decision-making and subsequent behavior, wouldn't it be nice to learn how to be deliberate in framing your perspectives? Break your mind's default framing using the following methods.

1. When presented with a problem or message don't swallow it line, hook, and sinker! First, reframe the problem or message more than once if possible. Consider different reference points from where to frame and reframe the problem or message. Similar to using the invert model, frame the situation, statement,

or idea from a negative perspective if it is in the positive or frame it in a positive perspective if it is in the negative.

2. Start thinking in terms of the quality of the questions you ask. I began this chapter by saying *"you can only see what you want to see."* What you see, the solutions you get, the ideas that occur to you, or the answers you get all depends on the quality of the question you ask. So, when you are faced with options, ask yourself multiple questions before deciding. Picking the first option that occurs to you is acting based on autopilot or your default mode of thinking.

3. Be mindful of the context of your framing. Your thoughts can be misled if a statement or problem is worded wrongly. In the words of William Poundstone, "The stumbling block isn't the certainty effect per se. It's the way that smart people are influenced by mere words, by the way the choices are framed" (Poundstone, 2010).

4. One way to break free from default thinking (framing bias) is to understand that almost everyone you interact with has a different perspective about an issue even if you are both looking at the same issue. When you seek to understand other people's perspectives, it would help you to reframe a situation differently and

approach it with a better understanding.

5. Challenge your perspective! You can do this by encouraging contrary opinions and perspectives from the people around you. Let your colleagues, friends, and even spouse know that you are open to their honest views even if they are sharply in disagreement with yours. Renowned CEOs and captains of industries are known to surround themselves with people who think differently than them and this is one huge factor for their fewer mistakes and higher success rates.

Here are some practical steps you can take right now to begin to frame or reframe the situations in your life to help you tackle them with more zest and vigor.

1. Start to think of the work you do as a "calling" instead of a "job." Framing your work in this light can lead to more commitment, engagement, and a higher level of satisfaction.

2. We are more inclined to think more of what we are going to lose if a situation goes bad. Begin to see this as an advantage instead of a curse. That is to say, use your power of imagination to conjure up the worst-case scenario in your mind and begin to see all the negative impacts losing or failing can cause. Ask yourself if you can live with such negative impacts. I am not

suggesting that you engage in overgeneralization (making a situation worse than it actually is). I am simply urging you to apply an earlier mental model I touched on while sharing the story of Charlie Munger in the previous chapter. By looking at what you are likely to lose you are more likely to take steps to correct it to prevent it from happening.

3. Ask yourself if the status quo of your life (or any particular area of your life) is acceptable to you. Take a particular aspect of your life and flip it over; do you like what you see? For example, if you currently earn $500 per month, begin to ask yourself if that is the highest you can earn. Is this amount all that I am worth? Does this amount reflect my true capabilities and potentials? Can I not go beyond this amount? In other words, you are beginning to shift your frame from looking at the glass as half full to half empty. Before long, you will start thinking of ways to improve yourself to earn more money or diversifying your resources (time, money, and energy) to generate more income.

Why Deliberate Framing Works

Isn't the glass-half-empty analogy a negative viewpoint? Well, it depends on how you frame it! Negative and positive are our interpretations of neutral events. Remember that how information is presented can determine whether or not we think it is less negative. Besides, we tend to be more motivated by potential loss than by what we can potentially gain. This explains why many people tend to be contented with their life's status quo and will do all they can to keep it that way but will find it difficult to put in the required effort to go beyond their status quo. Usually, there is less motivation for striving to achieve a goal than there is for losing what you already have. Have you not heard the saying, "a bird in hand is worth two in the bush?" That is a perfect reflection of low self-motivation. And the reason is that they have accepted the perception that their glass is half full. That type of thinking or framing can keep you longer than necessary in your status quo – your comfort zone, even when the zone is no longer comfortable!

Deliberately framing your situation can mean the difference between chasing your goals and settling for your current lifestyle. Almost every man has dreams and aspirations, but the drive to pursue that dream and the ingenuity to think outside the box (of their peculiar mental model) is usually truncated by their perception of their current situation.

Framing your current level of success as "I have done well for myself" is likely to lead to contentment, relaxation, and letting down your guard (just for a tiny bit!), and eventually hitting a plateau. On the flip side, framing your current level of success as "There is still room for improvement" is more likely to keep your creative juices flowing. Have you wondered why great athletes break their own records? Have you wondered why successful businessmen and women keep outdoing themselves year after year? They refused to accept the perception that says there's no more world to conquer! They are continually in the process of framing their situations to make them want to achieve more than they have already achieved.

Framing does not work only for negative situations. You do not need to wait until a situation gets bad before you deliberately change how you perceive the situation. For example, you have put a lot of effort into your relationship and it is working out fine. You could frame that positive situation as "If I can do this much, I definitely can achieve far better results in other areas of my life!"

60

Chapter 3: Let's Do It Like This... Or Wait... Maybe...

24-year-old Kelvin read the end-user agreement written in small print. His mind raced with several questions. Should he click the Agree button and take the huge risk of investing his hard-earned money or should he just click the Cancel button? How many times has he come to this crossroad? He has lost count. His salary from his job seems to be constantly shrinking compared to his responsibilities. And now that his wife is expecting a second child, he desperately needs another source of income. He had taken the advice of investment gurus to save up and invest in real estate crowdfunding to give him extra income. Moreover, since that is a passive investment, it would not affect his demanding job. How long ago was that? It's been three long years, and he's gone from one investment to the other and doesn't have any significant profit to show for it. Initially, he'll have some early profits, but before long, all he'll be left with are irredeemable losses.

He had read several motivational and self-help books. He set goals and put in his best efforts towards achieving his goals. But somehow, there doesn't seem to be any light at the end of Kelvin's tunnel. He had considered giving up but with mounting responsibilities and his wife recently quitting her job to be a stay-at-home mom, Kelvin is back at giving real estate investments another shot. Would he succeed this time? What does he need to do to succeed? What would help him make better decisions?

Like Kelvin in the fictional story, a lot of us are faced with situations that force us into making decisions whether or not we are well-prepared to make them. Some of these decisions are good, while for many, the decisions are mostly bad. But that isn't the only problem. Usually, in retrospect, we would think we've learned our lessons and then try again only to be greeted with another round of failure resulting from more bad decisions than good ones. So, how do you, like Kelvin, make the right decisions? Of all the hundreds of questions buffeting your mind almost daily on different subjects of your life, how would you know the right answers to give and the right choices to make? What do you need to know to free yourself from the trap of second-guessing yourself and going, "let's do it like this... or wait... maybe...?" Is there some special secret formula for making the right decisions? What do famous and successful businessmen know and use that the average struggling man doesn't know?

All these are the focus of this chapter. We shall take a look at the lives of a few men who are renowned for their successes. But our focus is not going to be on their wealth; rather, we shall pay more attention to how they were able to rise from the ashes of their several failures. Because, whether we want to admit it or not, the majority of successful people recorded a lot of heart-wrenching failures before they became successful at their various ventures. At the end of this chapter, you will understand that while there is no beeline to success, there are, however, ways of thinking that can give you an "unfair" edge over others who simply burrow through life armed with only hope. First, let us begin by studying the common mistakes people like Kelvin (and perhaps you too) make in decision-making.

Common Mistakes in Decision-Making

Driven by Emotions (Rushing into Decisions)

When you are angry and depressed or elated and excited, your decisions at those moments may not be rational. You may be under what is known as emotional hijack (or amygdala hijack) – where your rational mind is overtaken by your emotional mind and makes you respond according to what you are feeling in the spur of the moment regardless of the long-term effect of your response. For example, you are in a good mood and you offer to make a substantial donation for a project that you don't really care about before you have time to think through your decision. Or saying hurtful words in haste without pausing to think about it because you are angry, and then those words change your relationship forever.

Whether it is in your professional or personal situations, rushing into making important decisions can be a huge mistake. Jumping at the first alternative may not usually result in the best decision. Equally, making decisions without understanding the ramifications can be disastrous.

To avoid this, always hold off making decisions until you are in a reasonably stable state where you can think more clearly. You can deliberately take yourself out of such emotionally charged situations (take a walk or do something unrelated to the situation) to allow you to think more rationally.

Procrastination

Making a decision can be a difficult process sometimes. To avoid this difficulty, many people simply postpone making the decision and get along with the seemingly simple things that don't require too much thinking (their default way of living). However, what many people don't realize is that deciding to postpone a decision is a decision in itself. The longer you postpone an important decision, the more difficult it gets to rationally make up your mind especially when making the decision becomes critical.

Part of the reason for postponing a decision is the fear of

making mistakes. Own your decisions once you've made it. You may not get it right the first time, but mistakes show that you are attempting something instead of idling away in procrastination. Don't wait until you have to make a decision. Decide when you can boldly say, "I choose to."

Narrow-Mindedness

This is where selective perception and confirmation bias discussed in the previous chapter comes into play. Not giving your mind enough room to think beyond your current level of perception can lead to huge mistakes in decision-making. For example, you are excited about a new change you want to make in your business. Four out of your 15 employees seem happy about the change, so you go ahead with implementing the change regardless of the opposing ideas raised by the remaining 15. Your mind was already made up and you were merely seeking confirmation for your bias instead of seeking honest input.

To overcome narrowmindedness and biases, make sure that you are not making important decisions based on a single component without duly considering the bigger picture. Acknowledging your personal bias and your inexperience about the issue at hand will ensure that you keep things in perspective. Keep channels for new information open – avoid shooting from the hip! Gather relevant information and consider them first even if they seem opposed to your current perception. You may not accept the opposing views, but they can give you fresh insights on how to think inversely as successful people do.

The Halo Effect

Like Kelvin, many of us listen to gurus the way younger children learn from parents, adults, and society – with our minds wide open to receive and act without scrutiny. Making important decisions based on what someone you hold in high regard tells you may not work well at all times. It is similar to confirmation bias except that this is more about people. Once someone has given you a few good pieces of advice in the past or is known to make sound judgments, we tend to take in everything they say hook, line, and sinker.

Be open to advice from credible sources, but also think for yourself. Keep in mind that the person whose opinion you respect may not share your identical problem or situation for which you are trying to make the right decisions.

Overanalyzing

Analysis paralysis can occur from too much data to chew on. This stems from the desire to make perfect decisions. Overanalyzing will keep you focused on the trees while neglecting the forest! The big picture will be lost on you because your attention is engrossed in the details. Simply keep your eyes on relevant information that will give you useful clues of the future and not a bunch of historical data that only points to where you (and others) have been. Basing your decisions on outdated information can be fatal. Select a handful of factors that are critical and forget all other factors – they are mere distractions. If your decision proves to be wrong or does not go as expected, reexamine your factors and make adjustments.

Always remember that there will be room for improvement. You don't have to see the whole staircase before you take the first step. Your decisions don't have to be perfect from the outset. You can always adjust, improve, and improvise as you go along.

Do-or-Die Mentality

Approaching decision making with a do-or-die attitude often puts you under undue pressure. Kelvin, in our story, will find it difficult to make any rational decision in his current state of mind because he places his entire future on the click of one button! If you find yourself faced with a make-or-break decision, it is more than likely that you have made a series of bad decisions leading to that single decision. Usually, decisions made from this mentality are done to justify previous actions or to cover up past mistakes. In many cases, you will neglect your values (ignoring the right thing) while making this type of decisions.

Rationalizing Away Reality

Self-deceit is the worst form of deceit. Decisions made out of hope that current reality will bend to favor your decision is simply burying your head in the sand. No matter how unpleasant the realities on the ground are, you must take them into consideration while making your decisions. Kelvin would have to consider his financial standing, his growing responsibilities, and his current level of experience in real estate investing if he must make a sound decision. Ignoring his inexperience with regards to real estate investing in the hope that one single click will turn his fortunes around may be another financial disaster waiting to happen to him.

You need to be honest with yourself before making decisions, especially if they are important ones. I do not mean to offend your religious inclination or your belief in the supernatural, but I strongly suggest that you don't rely on hope or blind faith when making life-altering decisions. You have an inborn ability to reason – use it!

Okay, it's now time to examine the success stories of a few famous men. Remember to keep your attention on the mental models they used to achieve their successes.

Elon Musk: An Embodiment of First-Principle Thinking

Elon Musk is a highly successful and audacious entrepreneur who needs little or no introduction. His net worth of $19.3 billion as of 2019 is a clear testament to that fact. Musk has some lofty goals and visions among which are to significantly reduce global warming and establish a human colony on Mars to reduce the risk of human extinction (Anderson, 2014).

His successes cut across various fields from PayPal in the financial sector to Solar City (energy sector), SpaceX (aerospace), and Tesla Motors (automotive). These are all revolutionary companies that will change human history forever.

Apart from a series of failures, in both his personal and professional life, as well as being fired from his own company while on honeymoon, Mr. Musk was faced with challenges that would have made any other person succumb to the popular way of thinking. But not Elon; his success wasn't just as a result of his incredible work ethic. It is a result of his ability to think like a genius about his challenges.

But how does all this make any meaning to you? Here's how. Elon Musk was able to strip non-essentials from big ideas, challenges, and problems and then gradually work his way up in building a solution. This brings us to the first-principles thinking.

First-Principles Thinking

It isn't really about what Mr. Musk thinks that is the highlight of his success story. Instead, it is how he thinks about it. He simply doesn't accept that something should be done in a particular way because that's how it's always been done. He's really great at using the first-principles thinking to approach problems. So, what exactly is first-principle thinking? How did Elon Musk use it to solve problems? And most importantly, how can you use it in your life?

A first principle is a fundamental assumption or concept on which a method, formula, system, or theory is based. No further assumption can be reached beyond the first principle of a thing.

Let me put that in layman's terms. It is keenly questioning the assumptions you have about situations or problems and then building solutions about the problems and situations from scratch. This is how formulas and original solutions are derived – by stripping assumptions down to their fundamentals, to what is known as true, and then working back up.

One of Mr. Musk's multibillion-dollar companies, SpaceX,

came into existence through the conscious application of first-principles thinking. Elon wanted to send a rocket to Mars in 2002; however, there was a huge challenge which appeared insurmountable. The cost of buying a rocket was extremely high – in the range of $65 million. Instead of giving up the idea because of insufficient funds (like most will do), or postponing the idea of sending rockets to Mars until he can save up for the project at a later date, he began to question the generally held assumptions about rockets. He began taking the problem apart by asking what the basic components of a rocket are and the cost of those components or materials in the commodity market.

He found that rockets are made of materials like aerospace-grade aluminum alloys, carbon fiber, copper, and titanium. His quest also revealed that these materials are a lot cheaper in the commodity market, about 2% of the cost of a finished rocket! Instead of purchasing finished rockets, he bought the materials and built his own rockets. So, what appeared to be an insurmountable challenge turned out to be the birth of a new multimillion-dollar aerospace company!

This is the result of being guided by mental models that generate the right thinking. Using first-principles thinking, Musk was able to drastically cut down the cost of launching rockets while still making profits. He refused to settle for the assumption that rockets are astronomically expensive to launch and created a more effective solution.

How Does This Matter to You?

You may not be interested in developing innovative ideas, so how does using first-principle thinking apply to you? Well, for starters, it saves you from the trap of living by analogy instead of by thinking for yourself. Many people live by what can be best described as copy and paste. They see others doing things a certain way, and boom, they do the same without questioning the ideas, beliefs, and concepts. Sticking to old conventions and inherited ideas can limit your ability to think for yourself.

When you begin to take the time to consider how you approach your day-to-day problems, you may begin to find that you are merely regurgitating so-called solutions you inherited from others. We learned this from when we were kids. Parents and grownups will irritably respond with "Because I said so!" to our too many questions. As adults, we got the same answer, "Because that's how it's always been done!"

Equally, our analogical thinking makes us envisage future development using a current form instead of function. For example, critiques of technology may scoff at the idea of flying cars failing to see that flying cars are already in existence in the form of airplanes. The form may be different, but the function it serves (air transportation) is the same. In other words, for you to be more effective in decision-making, ask yourself what the functional outcome of what you are trying to accomplish is, and then make the best of the function without so much worry about the form.

Applying First-Principles Thinking in Your Life

Working with how others think means that we can only make incremental improvements. First-principles thinking means branching out from the norm and not living by analogies or conventions. Analogies are great – they help a cook, for example, to follow a recipe without bothering so much how the recipe came about. In that case, the analogy (recipe) saves the cook some time. However, the cook runs into problems when the situation requires a different dish. This is where a chef differs from a cook. The chef can think for himself and produce another recipe for the new dish. A cook is stuck without a recipe.

Thinking for yourself requires that you strip down assumptions to their basics. Here's how to do that.

1. Find out the genesis of your assumptions. What are your thoughts about a problem, challenge, or situation? Why do you think that way?

2. Challenge your assumptions. How do you know that what you think about a situation is true? Suppose you think the opposite?

3. Begin to look for evidence. Can you back up your thinking? What is the source of your evidence?

4. Seek other viewpoints. What do others think? How do you know that you are correct?

5. Consider the implications. What happens if I go wrong? What is at stake?

6. Cross-examine your earlier questions. Why did you think that way? Is that type of thinking correct? What have you reached from all your reasoning?

So, the next time someone says to you, "It's never been done before," take that as your cue to start striping down that assumption.

Ray Dalio: Decision Making with Second-Order Thinking

Ray Dalio, founder of Bridgewater Associates, the biggest hedge fund firm in the world is no doubt a successful investor and philanthropist. With a personal net worth of $19.4 billion in 2019, there's definitely a few principles of right-thinking we can learn from him with regards to life and work (Forbes,

2019).

As with many successful people, Ray Dalio had to learn through several mistakes and seeming failures. To him, there's a lot more to learn from failures than from success. He learned one of his most painful lessons when Mexico defaulted on his loans in 1982. Being a world-renowned successful hedge fund manager doesn't come without its own price! But how did Ray go from being almost completely broke to donating $768.9 million to different philanthropic causes? He changed his thinking, that's how. Instead of thinking, "I want this to be true!"; he started thinking, "How do I know this to be true?"

However, one of the major changes he applied to his thinking that resulted in a major shift in his life and fortune was the second-order thinking. When his market prediction came true, he went all in and made a huge financial decision based purely on first-order thinking without considering second-order thinking. His company tanked, and Ray had to borrow $4,000 from his dad at one time. He learned his lessons and made a comeback. Today, his company, which almost went under, now manages $160 billion.

What is Second-Order Thinking?

In simple terms, second-order thinking is a deliberate consideration of the consequences of your intended choices and decisions. It is thinking about possible future outcomes on more than one level before deciding on a course of action. It is a complex form of thinking. In contrast, first-order thinking is easy, considers only surface outcomes, and is commonly used.

Consider the following examples of first and second-order thinking:

1. Kelvin is trying to decide whether to invest in real estate, bonds, cash, stocks, or a mix? Currently, the market is on a downturn. Kelvin's first-order thinking would be something along the lines of, "Stay away from the markets! Investing is risky. The market is crashing, just save your money." If he's smart enough to think further, his second-order thinking would go, "The markets are currently down and that's making people panic. This means the stocks are a great bargain because they are grossly undervalued. I am still young and can take the risk. I'll invest."

2. A fat gangster, more than twice the size of Kelvin, is chasing him down a hallway. He gets to a staircase and has to decide whether to go up the stairs or down. "Go down. You'll move a lot faster when going down," screams first-order thinking. "Go up. You'll move slower but it'll be much more difficult for this thug to carry his weight up the stairs," says second-order

thinking.

3. Kelvin is trying to lose weight and eat healthily. First-order thinking will make him cringe at the thought of going to the gym, lifting weights, and passing on his favorite chocolate cakes. Second-order thinking will focus on the benefits of living healthier, stronger, and leaner.

More often than not, deciding and acting from first-order thinking cost us the very thing we want or block us from getting them. They are like temptations that distract from proper thinking. Athletes who use drugs to enhance their performance didn't give second-order thinking a chance. They only focused on the immediate results their decisions will bring (fame and fortune) without giving thought to the consequences of their actions if they are found out (a ban from sports participation, health hazards, and a ruined reputation). Lying to the people in your world can seem harmless and even make you achieve your agenda, but it is capable of destroying your relationships forever.

Avoiding Mediocrity

How can you outperform others and even your previous performance if you keep thinking the same way? To reach uncommon decisions, you need to think beyond the first easy level where almost everyone thinks. Mediocrity results from a common way of thinking and acting.

Your thinking processes have to take an unconventional form for you to stand out from the herd. Using second-order thinking can help you access ideas that are different and can also help you to process your ideas differently than the average person would.

Being Deliberate About Your Decisions

I'll like to suggest the following way through that you can apply second-order thinking in your day-to-day decisions.

1. Make a habit of asking yourself, "What happens next?" This opens your mind to think beyond the first-order thinking.

2. Try to think into the future and picture what the consequences of your decision would be in the short, medium, and long term.

3. Ask yourself how your decision will impact others and how they will respond. If it is a personal decision, how would your spouse or friend respond? If it is a business or career decision, how would your competition, employees, colleagues, or bosses respond?

Be wary of thoughts that immediately confirm your preconceived ideas or biases when you are faced with challenging situations. In Dalio's words,

"Failing to consider second- and third-order consequences is the cause of a lot of painfully bad decisions, and it is especially deadly when the first inferior option confirms your own biases. Never seize on the first available option, no matter how good it seems, before you've asked questions and explored." (Dalio, 2017)

Jeff Bezos: Thinking on Your Feet

Have you ever bought anything on Amazon, maybe this book? If you have, you have transacted business with Jeff Bezos! Even if you haven't bought anything on Amazon before, Jeff Bezos hardly needs any introduction. I mean, almost everyone knows the man who, in early 2019, was named the world's richest man with a net worth of $113 billion (Forbes, 2019).

Mr. Bezos couldn't have successfully built an incredible company like Amazon that generates more than $24 billion annual revenue, hire the right kind of people to run his businesses, and amassed an incredible fortune for himself without knowing and applying a few mental hacks that the ordinary man usually overlooks or is completely ignorant of.

Deciding Before You Decide

So, how do Jess Bezos and other successful people do it? In a world of constantly moving pieces, how do they know which piece will fit for what part of their personal and professional lives? Of all the several decisions they have to make, how do they know which is right and which is not? Well, first of all, successful people know that they don't have to make the right decisions at all times. This is one thing that keeps most people stuck; we want every decision we make to be the right one, and that explains why we don't easily change our minds. Because we have invested a lot of time, energy, and emotion into the decision, we want it to be right at all costs.

Here's what Bezos and other successful people do. They classify decisions into two broad categories.

Category 1: These are decisions that are almost irreversible. For example, quitting your job or selling your business. You will have to permanently live with the outcome of these types of decisions.

Category 2: These are decisions that can be easily reversed. A lot of the decisions you make daily fall into this category.

Erroneously assuming that all decisions are extremely important can keep you stuck longer than necessary. To improve your productivity and increase your worth before your boss, colleague, friends, or spouse, you need to be able to think on your feet. Taking too much time to make up your mind shows that you consider every decision as a Category 1 decision. It also shows that you desperately want to be right straight out of the bat! Doing that is essentially depriving yourself of the opportunity to learn from your experiences.

Successful people are not afraid of making a lot of decisions daily. It doesn't mean they've become so good that they don't make mistakes. It simply means they are willing to learn from their mistakes. For the highly successful leaders, business owners, athletes, entertainers, and so on, success comes with making a lot of mistakes. To the rest who are very careful to avoid mistakes, well, let's just say, being too careful is a sure path to a mediocre life.

So, the next time you need to make a decision, first decide if it is a Category 1 or 2 decision. You are not going to get all your decisions right and that is perfectly okay. The more you quickly make and execute Category 2 decisions, the faster you gather experience and understand how to make better decisions. Over time, the quality of your decisions will improve significantly.

Changing Your Mind… Quickly

Mr. Bezos was able to quickly change his mind when necessary because he believes that consistency of thought isn't necessarily a positive trait. If something is not working, change your mind! You are not stuck with one pattern of thinking. If you are confused as to whether you are stuck in the same pattern of thinking, carefully examine your results. It was Einstein who defined insanity as doing the same thing over and over again yet expecting a different result. You definitely cannot solve a problem with the same mindset that created the problem in the place.

Successful people don't cling onto a decision even when circumstances have changed. They are very flexible and quick to change their minds when they have ample evidence that suggests they are wrong. Perhaps that was one of Steve Jobs' great qualities. He understood that it was pointless holding unto an assumption in the face of changing circumstances. Tim Cook, Apple CEO had this to say about Steve Jobs,

"Steve would flip on something so fast that you would forget that he was the one taking the 180-degree polar opposite position the day before. I saw it daily. This is a gift, because things do change, and it takes courage to change. It takes courage to say, 'I was wrong.' I think he had that." (Cook, 2012)

The Mirage of Definite Thinking

You must develop the habit of continually revising your understanding especially if a problem you thought you had solved keeps resurfacing. Nothing can get you more stuck than trying to be always definite in your decisions. It keeps you fixated on all the seemingly important details you need to sort through while neglecting the big picture of the situation at hand. You must give up the need to be right all the time.

So, don't be afraid to make decisions because you don't want to go wrong. Going wrong or failing on Category 1 decision only makes you wiser. This is what Jeff Bezos has to say on failing,

"Failure and invention are inseparable twins. To invent you have to experiment, and if you know in advance that it's going to work, it's not an experiment. Most large organizations embrace the idea of invention, but are not willing to suffer the string of failed experiments necessary to get there."

Did I mention how many times Elon Musk attempted a rocket launch and failed? Did I mention the millions of dollars he lost on each of those failed attempts? I would rather leave those details to your imagination. But failure didn't stop Mr. Musk from refining and making better decisions either.

More Mental Models for Making Better Decisions

The Bayesian Thinking

The work of Thomas Bayes, an 18th century English minster led to what is known as Bayesian thinking. In simple terms, this is the core of Bayesian thinking. When you encounter new information or learn something new, you should take into account your prior relevant knowledge and how it validates or negates the new information. Given that a lot of your prior information and knowledge are useful, you shouldn't simply discard them because you learn something new. Equally, given that we in a constantly changing world, you shouldn't discard new information because it contradicts your prior information. This means you should take into consideration all prior relevant information (what statisticians call a base rate) when making decisions. There are a lot of statistical analysis and calculations that can be used to arrive at probabilities of things being true or not, but I will not bore you with such computations. My goal is to help you apply this and the other mental models in the decisions you encounter in your daily life and not to take you through the hypothetical processes of these models.

Bayesian thinking is particularly useful when you are faced

with making decisions involving uncertain situations or predicting a likely outcome. It is almost always a gross mistake to make decisions in uncertain situations without pausing to ask yourself what you may already know that can help you better understand the reality of the uncertain situation. For example, you invite a handyman to fix a broken faucet in your kitchen and he begins to snoop around the house. Later in the day, the local news reports a case where a repairman returned to a house where he had previously worked to rob. You are perplexed and begin to worry that this handyman may come back and rob you. You can go ahead with that assumption and begin to frantically take precautionary measures that can cost you time, money, and effort, or take a pause to apply the Bayesian thinking before taking any action in the uncertain situation.

To apply the Bayesian thinking to the above situation, start by asking how many times repairmen have been reported to rob a house and how likely is that to happen in this instance. Are you basing your fear on a single piece of evidence (the news report) or it is a frequent occurrence? How many repairmen are robbers and how many are honest? By relying on previous information and comparing it to the new information, you can determine the likelihood of the outcome, in this case, the repairman coming back to rob you or not. You can lock your doors or install alarm systems, but getting worked up over that piece of new information isn't the best use of your time and can push you into making poor decisions like calling the police to investigate an honest repairman.

You can apply Bayesian thinking in the workplace too. For example, a colleague named Sam, whom you suspect is envious one of your direct reports named Kelvin, begins to complain to you about Kelvin's poor attitude towards finishing a project. You can immediately confirm your earlier assumption that Sam is indeed envious of Kelvin, or take a pause and think about the situation. Is Sam in the habit of complaining about Kelvin or any other colleague for that matter? Is Kelvin actually being sluggish about the project? Is it out of place for a colleague to complain about another's poor work attitude? This line of questioning can help you better understand the reality of the situation without jumping to rash conclusions or leaning toward confirmation bias.

To help you remember how to use the Bayesian thinking, keep the following in mind when you are about to make a decision in an uncertain situation:

1. Remember the things you know prior to the new information.

2. Imagine that your conclusions are wrong. How would that affect your personal life, work, and others who are directly affected by that conclusion?

3. Review and update your knowledge incrementally.

Discarding everything you know about a situation prior to obtaining new information could prove fatal.

Loss Aversion

Would you expect a farmer to sit all day watching and waiting for a seed he planted to sprout? Definitely not! But many people do just that. When you take a quick peek at your investment for the umpteenth time in one day, for example, or when you continuously check on your new romantic partner to be sure that their feelings for you haven't changed, you are like the farmer urging his seeds to grow! The reason we do that is that the pain we feel by losing something is far more than the pleasure we feel by getting it.

In Chapter 2, I mentioned that many people would prefer to maintain their current status than putting in the required effort to attain a higher status. This is because of what psychologists call loss aversion. We hate losing. But how does that affect our ability to make more right decisions? The more you see losses, the greater the psychological pain you experience, and the higher your chances of making a bad decision especially during worst and challenging times.

I could go into all the theories and details of scientific research on how our brains are affected and react to the several stimuli we get about perceived losses and gains but that may not be very beneficial to you. What I am primarily concerned with is how this can help you improve the quality of decisions you make.

Whenever you are in a situation that requires you to present information to others (clients, customers, colleagues, family, friends, and so on), always remember that people are interested in less risk and more gains; people want to be assured of gains even when they are taking risks. Therefore, tailor your information to gains rather than losses, for example, offer discounts instead of surcharges or extra charges. Offer guarantees for product and services instead of caveats. Offer love and assurance instead of warnings and insinuated threats. However, if there is significant uncertainty in a situation, present the information, but don't focus too much on the possibility for failure or unpleasant outcomes. Be more focused on potential successes.

Reverse Thinking

We brought Chapter 1 to a close with a short story of Charlie Munger and how he used the reverse or invert thinking. Briefly, let us look at how you too can apply this mental model in your daily life.

Armed with the understanding that reverse thinking is simply looking at a problem from an inverted angle, here's a practical example on how to use it in a work situation:

1. Firstly, define the problem you are trying to solve. For example, your sales are significantly falling and you are trying to increase it.

2. The next step is to invert the problem. Think from the reverse angle instead of how to solve it. What exactly do you need to do to ensure that the situation gets worse? How can you take a great product or service and make sure that it doesn't sell? You may begin to consider things like, making the buying process very complex, using a cheap and unreliable computer program, web service, or app for the sales, not making enough cold calls or downplaying the role of advertising campaigns, offering only one type of payment method, not providing adequate customer support, and so on.

3. The final step is to see how to avoid the pitfalls you have identified in Step 2.

Here's another example that shows how you could apply this in your personal life. Suppose you are trying to improve your relationship with your teenager. Think of what would guarantee that the relationship grows worse?

- Infrequent communication.

- Talking to your teenager only when he or she has done something wrong.

- Spending little to no time with them.

- Not being there for them and not taking an interest in their activities.

- Breaking your promises to them.

- Putting them down in front of their peers.

Working to avoid these things is an easier way to guarantee a healthier relationship with your teenager than spending time worrying over how to improve the relationship.

When you begin to feel stuck about how to move forward, perhaps it is time to start thinking about how to go backward or how to not go forward – invert, always invert!

Bottom Line

There is something about success that is undeniably connected to failure. Unfortunately, when we think of famous people, our attention is usually on their results without much consideration for the series of failures they went through and the mental toughness that saw them through the tough times. Of course, they are financially successful people who didn't have to go through massive failures to become wealthy, and if you are born with the proverbial silver spoon, then money struggles may sound alien to you. However, success is not only about money and fame. Failure can also be in relationships, bad habits, health and fitness, and so on.

When you encounter setbacks in any aspect of your life, think more about how a shift in perspective can help you and less about how much of a failure you are. Easier said than done, I know, but that's how successful people think. They get knocked down more times than they care to admit but still get back up. Your name may not make the list of top 100 successful men of your time (and that may not even be your goal), but you definitely are successful if you can understand and apply the wisdom shared by these highly successful men.

Chapter 4: This Can Be Done Faster…

How can you shorten the time it takes for you to do the things you do without compromising quality? Better still, how can you significantly improve productivity and at the same time drastically cut down the time you put into your work? How do you optimize your productivity to achieve over-the-top success?

For many people, the answer would be to develop an incredible work ethic, but that would mean putting in more hours in your work and can lead to burnouts. While I am totally for having a healthy work ethic, I do not subscribe to the thinking that suggests that you need to work long hours to be efficient and more productive.

A small business owner can pour all his efforts and waking hours into his business project, but working round the clock as an entrepreneur cannot yield greater and better results than a competitor who can assemble a team to handle a similar project in far less time because the team can collectively put in more man-hours. That is one way to work smarter instead of harder. The entrepreneur may be busy throughout his waking hours, but being busy doesn't necessarily translate into being productive. As Adam Grant, author of *Give and Take*, puts it,

"If you want something done, ask a busy person. The old saying rings true, but it also spells doom for that busy person" (Grant, 2014).

However, improving productivity isn't just about managing your time alone. It also involves effectively managing your energy – spending less and less of your energy while still generating the maximum benefits possible. What other ways can you work smarter instead of harder and longer? The answer to that and the previous questions are what this chapter is designed to answer using mental models that can help you improve efficiency. But first, let's take a brief look at what most people do that prevents high productivity.

Thing You Do That Prevents Productivity

Working Overtime

As earlier mentioned in the preceding paragraphs, working for longer hours does not automatically equal higher productivity. If anything, working for longer hours tends to reduce your productivity because you are susceptible to burnouts. When are you likely to have brilliant ideas and clear insights? Is it when you are buried in your work with your mind and body all worked up or when your mind and body are relaxed, calm, and off from desperately trying to figure out how to solve a problem?

Not Having Adequate Sleep

Do you bring work back home? Do you take your gadgets (phones, tablets, laptops, and so on) to bed? Do you deprive yourself of adequate sleep in a bid to get a head start on the next day's tasks? If you do any of these, you shouldn't be surprised if your productivity isn't getting any better. Sleep recharges your body and mind – both of which you need to be efficient at work. Great leaders and successful people all maintained a habit of having adequate sleep because they understand the immense benefit it gives your body and all its various systems. Some great minds and leaders even included napping during the day as part of their daily routine. Leonardo da Vinci, Thomas Edison, Winston Churchill, President John F. Kennedy, President Ronald Reagan, John D. Rockefeller, and many other successful people are known for sleeping for short periods during the day (Hyatt, 2016).

Allowing Distraction

What does your computer screen look like – cluttered with icons, completely iconless, or having a couple of icons? How many tabs do you have opened at the same time on your computer? How about your phone, how many apps do you have installed and how many do you actually use? Modern life comes with its blessings and curses, heavy distraction being one of them. You cannot expect your productivity to improve if you are constantly distracted by your gadgets. To help get you less distracted, unclutter your computer and phone; only keep programs and apps that are really useful to you. Turn off your phone or turn off all notifications until you are through with your tasks.

Saying Yes to Irrelevant Tasks Too Often

Usually, no one wants to be seen as the bad guy so we are inclined to agreeing to tasks that are irrelevant to the results we seek. When you give people the impression that you are responsive to every request, you open yourself up to a flood of never-ending requests and saying no becomes difficult. Before saying yes to a task, take the time to evaluate whether it can lead to greater productivity or it would just be a waste of your time and energy. In the next section when we explain the mental models that can improve our productivity, we shall take a look at the Pareto principle to determine what to say yes to and what to say no to. But for now, suffice it to quote Warren Buffett on saying "no" as stated on the BBC Worklife website: "The difference between successful people and very successful people is that very successful people say 'no' to almost everything" (BBC, 2014).

Doing Everything Yourself

One of the number one causes of burnout is trying to do everything yourself. When you fail to ask for help or build a system that makes your work more efficient you are slowing down yourself, using up more of your time and energy, and ignoring the leverage that can significantly increase your productivity. If there are tasks you repeat often, it is in your best interest to seek ways to automate that task to save yourself time, energy, and money. Automation and building a system is more efficient than multitasking because multitasking does not allow you to give your very best to any individual task. Instead, your attention is scattered all over the place trying to do everything at the same time. You do not know everything, nor should you try to. There principle known as the Circle of Competence (more on this later). Become good at what you do, even if it is just one thing, but allow others who are also good at what they do to assist you to attain your goals more efficiently than only you could ever do.

Trying to Get It Right the Very First Time

It is okay to put your best effort into your work, but you should not become obsessed with perfection that you waste valuable time on trying to get things done perfectly from the very onset. The more attention to pay to perfectionism the lesser your productivity because you are focused on the nitty-gritty and paying less attention to the big picture, you spend too much time than required on problems and tasks, and you are always waiting for the perfect moment. There is no perfect moment to execute an idea than now. If you ever find a so-called perfect moment, you can be sure you are already too late!

Relying on Guesswork

Making decisions without having reliable data is taking unnecessary risk. You cannot optimize productivity and maximize efficiency through guesswork. Taking time to do your research will save you a lot of pains, regrets, and wasted efforts. If you cannot find reliable data, you can examine your own results and determine what the best cause of action would be.

The next two sections of this chapter are focused on mental models that can help you optimize your productivity and improve your systems. Note that these mental models are not limited to only these two functions. I have only categorized them this way for the purpose of convenience, logic, and the flow of this book. They are very much applicable to other areas of life. Let me quickly add here that using mental models the way a kid in school recites his multiplication table is not the proper use of mental models. Your ability to know which mental model to use for any given situation shows your true knowledge and understanding of its function. As Charlie Munger puts it in his 1994 speech entitled, *A Lesson on Elementary Worldly Wisdom*:

"Well, the first rule is that you can't really know anything if you just remember isolated facts and try and bang 'em back. If the facts don't hang together on a latticework of theory, you don't have them in a usable form. You've got to have models in your head. And you've got to array your experience both vicarious and direct on this latticework of models. You may have noticed students who just try to remember and pound back what is remembered. Well, they fail in school and in life. You've got to hang experience on a latticework of models in your head." (Munger, 1994)

Mental Models for Optimizing Productivity

Circle of Competence

"I'm no genius. I'm smart in spots, but I stay around those spots" (Tom Watson Sr., Chairman, and CEO of IBM, 1914 – 1956).

The things you think you know are quite different from the things you know. If you build your life around the things you think you know, you may find that you are like the proverbial jack-of-all-trades who is incompetent in any of the trades. The circle of competence simply means that we all have areas where our knowledge and skills have been fully developed through experience and through some study. We are good at some things but not everything. Building your work and life around those areas where you are very competent will guarantee high productivity.

Perhaps the story of Thomas Watson Sr., the former CEO of IBM between the years 1914 to 1956, explains the idea of the Circle of Competence more clearly. After working for only one day as a teacher, he gave up the job and went for a one year course in accounting and business (Wikipedia, n.d.). He took up a job as a bookkeeper in 1891 earning just about $6 a week. His first job as a salesman was selling pianos and organs and making about $10 weekly. Dissatisfied, he quit and began selling sewing machines for a while, then peddling loans, and then finally started a butcher shop which failed afterward. That left him broke, without a job or any investment.

Watson had gathered experience in sales and knew that if given the right opportunity, he would do well in sales. He saw that opportunity when he met John J. Range, the Buffalo branch manager of National Cash Register – one of the leading selling organizations of the mid-1800s. Watson persisted until he was hired by Range in 1896. Range mentored Watson into a fine salesman who became the most successful salesman in the East. His earnings went from a $10 to $100 a week. In 1914, Watson was hired as the general manager of Computing-Tabulating-Recording (CRT) Company and was made the president of the company after just 11 months. He doubled the company's revenue to $9 million, and in 1924, he renamed CRT to International Business Machines (IBM).

What are the takeaways from this story?

- Stick to what you are good at; you'll make more impact in your area of competence.

- If you keep jumping from one method of doing things to the other, you'll waste a lot of time and energy. Get good at applying a few important methods and your productivity will shoot through the roof.

- You may have the basic ideas of doing a thing and want to improve on it. That's okay. Devote time and energy to the learning of skills that will make you more productive.

- Don't be afraid to say you don't know a thing if you don't know it. However, if knowing it will greatly improve your odds of success in life, you should go ahead and learn it.

- Define a clear perimeter of your competencies and keep yourself within that perimeter. Gradually increase that perimeter over time to include areas that are absolutely necessary for your success.

- Never fool yourself into assuming that you can do a thing if it doesn't fall into your clearly defined perimeter.

Bottom line: Identify the area or a few areas where you are great and apply your most effort there. You will accomplish more and achieve greater things by limiting your focus to your circle of competence while allowing others who are skillful to compliment you in the areas you know little to nothing about.

Pareto Principle (The 80/20 Rule)

Do you find yourself busy all day long but accomplish far less than the efforts you put into your activities? If that is the case, your unsatisfactory accomplishments are not an indication that you are lazy or not putting in the required effort. It, however, indicates that you are giving your effort to tasks that have low value or impact on your overall output. In most cases, you are assigning the same amount of importance to all your tasks and activities instead of focusing on only the very few that are guaranteed to double your output.

If you live your life by inverting the principle of garbage in, garbage out such that you put in your best efforts into every single activity that comes your way, perhaps it is time you considered modifying attitude a little bit with the Pareto principle which is also known as the 80/20 rule.

The Pareto principle states that about 20% of all causes results in about 80% of all effects. In simple terms, this means that of all your activities, only about 20% of these will account for about 80% of your results.

To break this down a bit further, if you itemize 10 things on your daily to-do list, only about two items on that list will have the greatest positive impact on your day in comparison to the other eight items put together. Given this to be true, wouldn't it be wise to prune your activities to the most vital and then give more attention and energy to those since they yield the greatest results?

The important thing in the 80/20 rule is not the exact percentage but that you should understand that in very many cases, a cause is not directly proportional to effect. This is especially true for productivity; a relatively small proportion of the causes (effort, time, attention, manpower, and tasks) usually yield the most effects.

The Pareto principle is applicable in almost every area of life. For example, only a small portion of your customers will account for a greater percentage of the total revenue your business generates. Recognizing these customers and paying more attention to satisfying their needs can significantly improve your revenue. The key to using this principle is for you to find out the primary cause of a particular result and then optimizing the result using the primary cause.

World-renowned motivational speaker and self-development author, Brian Tracy, shared an interesting story on his blog that captures the essence of the 80/20 rule. It was about one of his friends who wanted to double his income within three to five years using the Pareto principle (Tracy, 2018). The friend found that he spends equal amounts of time on both his high- and low-profit clients. He gave all his clients the same level of energy and devotion. On discovering the 80/20 rule, he carefully examined his client base and separated the high-profit clients from the low-profit clients. As expected, only a small percentage of his client base fell into the high-profit group, leaving the larger percentage in the low-profit group.

What the friend did next was both decisive and life changing. He called in other professionals in his field and politely, strategically, and carefully handed off the low-profit clients (who represented only 20% of his business) to them. Next, he concentrated his energy and best efforts on the remaining smaller percentage that represented 80% of his business profits. He also began searching exclusively for new clients who matched the profile of his high-profit clients. His goal was to find those whom he could offer high-quality service in return for high profits.

The result of this move was incredible. Instead of achieving his goal of doubling his income in three to five years, his income doubled in only one year of using the Pareto principle to manage his time and energy.

We can also see something similar to the 80/20 principle in the story of Mike Flint, the personal pilot of Warren Buffett. Flint wanted to clearly define his career priorities, so he could maximize his focus and master his priorities. Mr. Buffett offered a two-step process for him to achieve his goal.

1. He asked Mike to write down 25 of his top career goals, which Flint did.

2. He asked Mike to carefully review the list and then circle out five of the most important goals from that list and have them as his second list. Mr. Flint complied as directed.

Mike Flint was determined to immediately start working on his second list – the top five most important of his career goals. Then, Mr. Buffett asked what he intends to do with his first list of top 20 items. Mr. Flint said his top five list is his primary target, but he'll give his attention to the list of top 20 items from time to time as he sees fit. At this point, Mr. Buffett gave him the most important lesson of the two-step process. He told Mr. Flint never to pay any attention to the list of 20 items and to avoid that list at all cost until he accomplishes his top 5 most important goals.

The lesson? Eliminating unnecessary activities will help you maximize your focus and energy. The activities that yield little to no results appear important to us unless we take time to thoroughly evaluate and handpick the ones that actually lead to greater results.

Here are some key points to keep in mind:

- A large number of your unproductive activities take up most of your time and energy. Invert this, and you'll figure out what tasks you need to focus on.

- Usually, tasks that produce the greatest positive impact appear the hardest. Tackle them first because the payoff for accomplishing them outweighs the results of accomplishing a multitude of other valueless tasks. Stop postponing your valuable tasks for the day.

- Doing many small irrelevant tasks is more appealing than tackling one or two major tasks. Don't give in to the temptation of clearing the irrelevant task first. As Brian Tracy puts it, look for the biggest frog and eat it first.

- Also, not all mental models will generate the greatest

impact on your life. Find those that are really relevant to your goals and lifestyle and then apply them constantly.

Bottom line: Not everything in your life and work deserves equal attention and effort. To significantly reduce busying around and eventually improve your overall productivity, use the Pareto principle to discover the tasks and activities that have the greatest impact on both your personal and professional life and then concentrate your time, money, and energy on those activities.

Minimum Viable Product (MVP)

Have you seen the number of useless mobile apps on app stores lately? They are all representative of someone's idea that was not tested before launching into the market. Those apps were developed on the assumption that there was a need for their use in the marketplace. Time and effort were put into their development, but it didn't meet user's needs and, therefore, didn't sell as expected. Instead of an increase in productivity, the developers experienced the exact opposite. But no developer has failed unless he or she gives up on their idea and refuses to go back to the drawing board to trace where the error lies. The higher your ability to quickly detect your errors, the faster you will be at correcting and making necessary adjustments. This is an important fact to keep in mind when trying to improve productivity, go into any creative venture, or start up a new business.

Contrary to what the name suggests, a minimum viable product is not necessarily a product at all. Instead, it is a process for testing your ideas and assumptions to ensure that there is an actual need for your idea (and product).

The MVP test process can be broken into two tests.

1. The first test is to determine what your riskiest assumption is.
2. The second is to figure out the smallest and simplest experiment that can put the assumption to test.

If you don't use the MVP process especially when coming up with some new idea, you may discover to your utter dismay that you've wasted energy, money, and a whole lot of time on an idea that is of no benefit to anyone. For example, before devoting several months into designing and developing a mobile app, a business idea, or even a lifestyle change for yourself and your spouse, test whether or not others are interested in that idea. Go round your potential app users or whatever idea it is you are developing and figure out if there is a need for what you want to create. If there is none, it may be a bit heartbreaking, but you have saved yourself time, energy, and money. If there is a need for your idea, the MVP process continues in small increments until your product or idea is matured and has a steady growth.

No matter the current level of your productivity, there is no harm in going back to the drawing board and using the MVP process to optimize your productivity. Remember that testing your ideas is a continuous process, regardless of whether it is in your personal or work life.

For many successful people, their success usually began with failure. But they understood something very important, and it was that failure is feedback. One of such people is Bill Gates, founder of Microsoft, multiple times world's richest man, and currently the second richest man on earth with a net worth of $103.7 billion (Forbes, 2019). Gates first company known as Traf-O-Data failed. As a matter of fact, during the first demo of that business, the machine didn't work! Gates, alongside his business partner, Paul Allen, went back to the drawing board and continued testing their ideas and assumptions until Microsoft was born.

But for some other people, success begins with a failing streak! Such was the case of Sir James Dyson, the British inventor with a net worth of $5.4 billion (Forbes 2019). His first, second, and up to 5,127 prototypes for a bag-less vacuum all failed. Talk about sticking to your vision! Dyson is a modern-day Thomas Edison who didn't consider his many failed attempts as failures but 10,000 ways his ideas won't work. Dyson went back to the drawing board each time he failed until he got it right. In his words, "There are countless times an inventor can give up on an idea. By the time I made my 15th prototype, my third child was born. By 2,627, my wife and I were really counting our pennies. By 3,727, my wife was giving art lessons for some extra cash. These were tough times, but each failure brought me closer to solving the problem" (Dyson, 2003).

Bottom Line: While it may be great to stick to your ideas and work relentlessly to come up with something that is of benefit to you and others, you can avoid the colossal waste of time and resources by testing your idea with incremental development steps.

Division of Labor

That no one can do everything on their own is no new knowledge; in spite of this, we still fall into the trap of trying to accomplish everything on our own. Imagine a large household where only the mother goes about doing everything from cleaning to laundry and cooking, mowing the grass, taking out the trash, and just about all the house chores. Other members of the household would become redundant and the mother would be worn out. Over time, her overall output will start to decline due to continuous burnout.

Unfortunately, this scenario can play out at work especially if you have a small business or you are a startup. It is expected that over time, startups expand to hire more manpower to allow for division of labor and division of work. The two are similar but not the same.

Division of labor means separating work into different tasks, roles, and steps which ultimately results in specialization. Division of work refers to breaking down work into different tasks with the goal of scaling yourself and your business. Nevertheless, both are often used interchangeably. For the purpose of this book, I use both meanings when I refer to division of labor.

I do not intend to lecture you on this fundamental principle of economics, so we shall not go into the nitty-gritty of it. All the same, if you can put this one principle to work in your professional endeavor, you will begin to see significant improvement in your productivity because you are not just dividing work, but you are equally building an efficient and interdependent system. By allowing people to handle different aspects of your work, they will specialize in those areas and form a formidable team of experts.

On the flip side, having just one person that is the go-to guy for every aspect of your business is not healthy for your business even if the go-to guy is yourself. Self-sufficiency is not a positive trait when it comes to running a business that involves hiring other employees. Instead of leading to greater output, it causes burnout, overdependence on one person, and redundancy among the others.

Applying the principle of division of labor can also be in the form of asking for help. This is particularly true if you are an employee. Don't bury yourself under a mountain of tasks working yourself to stupor just to complete them alone. Even if you are an expert in your field, learn to delegate some tasks (if you have the power to do so) or ask for help from others. Arrogance is a negative trait that can prevent you from asking for help. Arrogant people will prefer to suffer silently than simply ask for help. If you are in business, arrogance can cost you a lot of money!

Asking for help lightens your workload, gives you time off from work to do other equally important things, decreases your stress level, and gives you the time you need to get out of your own way.

Perhaps one of the leaders who masterfully demonstrated the use of division of labor was Henry Ford, who, at the time of his death, was worth $100 million (Forbes, 2017). Before Ford's advancement in automobile production, cars were previously produced by craftsmen. Typically, the craftsmen are highly skilled individuals who are very knowledgeable about every aspect of cars including the physics of cars, design, mechanics, metallurgy, engineering, and so on. Many of the craftsmen could build a car from scratch to finish by themselves – they were that good.

Then came Ford with his assembly line, which is basically the division of labor. He put together a small team that designed cars as well as map out the assembly process. Then another team – a larger one built the cars. Usually, the larger team is made up of both skilled and unskilled workers. The process was so simple that just about anyone can be included in the larger team to help build a car even if they are so uninformed that they have never seen a car before!

The entire process was faster, more efficient, cost less, and increased the production of cars. Also, there was no clash or overlap of knowledge and skills. Each person knows only what he needs to do his job well and that was sufficient to accomplish the task. There was no need for any single assembly worker to know every detail about building cars. In fact, an assembly worker could focus only on building wheels without knowing what a complete car looks like – as long as he can screw parts together, he'll be okay. This lead to specialization as each worker gets used to his part of the work and that in turn led to a higher quality of job output.

Bottom Line: Your work and personal life get easier if you apply the principle of division of labor. Allow others to do what they do best and focus on specializing in what you do best. That is a more efficient way to live.

Incentives

Incentives are rewards that are used to motivate people. The concept is built on the idea that we are likely to do what is in our own best interest. Providing the right incentive can alter how people behave. The key phrase here is the right incentive. Finding the right incentive requires that you know exactly what will motivate people and then aligning what you intend to achieve with what will motivate them. For example, a parent promises to buy his child their favorite toy if they got good grades. The child is interested in getting the new toy so they'll concentrate more on their schoolwork and perform better because they want the reward.

As adults, our motivations differ, but there's one common motivator among many adults, and that is money. Promise an employee a promotion or a raise, and he'll be willing to put in extra efforts in his job. This was clearly demonstrated by FedEx employees who were supposed to handle overnight shipping services. Initially, it was difficult for FedEx to keep up with delivery schedules because employees moving packages from one plane to the next wasn't fast enough, and the planes were delayed.

To solve this problem, FedEx introduced an incentive. It was no longer going to be "payment per hour" but "payment per shift." That means that no matter the number of hours the employees moving packages put in, their pay would remain the same. In other words, they could finish their work sooner and go home, yet be paid the same amount. The night shift employees saw no reason why they shouldn't work faster and FedEx got what it desired – an efficient overnight shipping service. It was a win-win situation for all.

Non-monetary incentives can also be used to boost productivity in your business. A very good example of aligning incentives with your goals can be seen in the Lambda School cofounded by Austen Allred. What is spectacular about Lambda School is that it aligns its business ideas with the motivation of its students. Students who are accepted into the school's program don't pay a dime to the school until they graduate, and the school gets them a job that pays at least $50,000 annually. After this, the school can begin to deduct a small amount from their monthly income for up to two years (Indie Hacker, 2018).

But Austen Allred didn't just start Lambda School on a platter of gold. He had the misfortune of watching his business implode, and he ran into debts. He then began learning some life-transforming lessons that helped him put his entrepreneurial experience to good use and recovered his lost fortune at the same time help others change their lives with the Lambda School. And by the way, he learned those lessons from Charlie Munger and Jeff Bezos!

Okay, so should you start promising your employees mouth-watering rewards to get them triple your revenue? Well, incentives have to be right. If you overdo it to make people meet unrealistic goals, they may end up cutting corners and eventually jeopardize your business. This was the case with Wells Fargo when in 2016, the company was fined several millions of dollars for creating unauthorized accounts for clients without their consent (Shapiro, 2018). Wells Fargo employees wanted to meet unrealistic quotas, so they cut corners and landed the company in a financial scandal.

So, what are the takeaways from these stories?

- As a leader, you can modify the behavior of your group to achieve your goals if you carefully align your goals with the incentives you offer to your group.

- Be sure to be clear on what you want if you are using incentives to motivate employee performance. Let them know that you are interested in increased revenue generation, but not to the detriment of the company.

- Money is a great way to motivate people, but it certainly is not the only way to offer incentives.

- You can combine incentives with loss aversion power to increase the chances of compliance. For example, instead of positively motivating an employee, you could imply that certain privileges will be withdrawn if they fail to meet a goal.

Bottom Line: Others are likely to put in more effort if they have the right level of motivation. Use that right level of motivation to steer them towards your goal.

Mental Models for System Thinking

KISS Principle

What better model to start with than one which teaches the simplicity of a system? KISS is an acronym for Keep It Simple Stupid. It originated back in 1960 when Kelly Johnson, an American aeronautical and systems engineer, handed a few tools to his team of engineers and challenged them to keep the design of the jet aircraft they were building simple such that an average mechanic under combat conditions can repair the aircraft with only those tools (Wikipedia, n.d.). This KISS principle does not imply stupidity; rather, it means keeping system designs simple, while being able to perform functions optimally, is the best form of sophistication.

You don't have to be an engineer or a mechanic to use the KISS principle. Here's how you can apply it to your life and work to optimize productivity.

1. **Time Management:** It is easy to feel overwhelmed when you want to do everything at the same time

because your mind is focused on the complexity of handling and accomplishing multiple tasks within the shortest possible time. KISS the overwhelmed feeling by making a list of the things you need to do in their order of importance and begin to prioritize them. As you complete tasks, cross them off the list to give you a sense of accomplishment.

2. **Relationships:** Keep your relationships with others very simple by taking what they say at face value. Stop wasting your time and energy on trying to figure out if they have some hidden agenda. Simply accept their truth and move on with your life. Also, say the things you mean, and mean the things you say. Stop complicating your communication; it's a sheer waste of time.

3. **Problem Solving:** If you identify a problem, don't wait for someone else to resolve it. Even if you can't fix it or is not your job to fix it, you can take steps to resolve it by simply pointing it out. If you let mind games to encroach into your work, it will complicate issues that can be resolved long before it became critical.

4. **Sending Messages:** Whether it is hand-written, text, verbal, or by email, be concise. Leave out unnecessary details. It saves valuable time for everyone. Also, it

prevents miscommunication.

5. **Work and Life Balance:** To enjoy personal or family life and your work life, there must be a clear boundary between the two. Focus on your work when it is time for work. Keep work out of your family or personal time. Don't complicate things by mixing the two – it doesn't result in more productivity. Instead, creating and respecting the boundary between the two can lead to productivity at work and a happier version of you and your family life.

6. **Health:** Instead of fussing over what diet to choose, simply asking yourself what types of food are healthier will point you in the right direction. Exercising doesn't necessarily have to be in a fancy gym. What physical activities do you enjoy doing? These are things that can easily be your form of exercise.

Bottom line: It doesn't make your personal life or work life easier to complicate things. Whether it is a process, system, or a technique for doing a thing, always remember this: keep simple tasks as simple as possible. The ultimate form of sophistication is simplicity.

Checklist

Imagine setting up your projector and screen for an important business presentation and then realizing that you forgot to bring along the projector cord! Failing to close a deal because you forgot something as small as a cord may not be that much of a big deal – you could close a better deal the very next day, but forgetting a surgical tool inside a patient you operated or operating the wrong body part (yes, it happens) can lead to serious complications, irreparable damages, and even death.

Question: Why do we forget the most common things? Why do we for routine tasks that we repeat even almost daily?

Short answer: We have limited memory and attention.

Long answer: Complex tasks, repetitive tasks, and tasks that involve too many steps tend to be difficult for our brain to remember from start to finish. It is not that we do not know what should be done, but it is our brain's inability to retain every single detail of what needs to be done.

This is why a checklist is a powerful tool in that it stimulates thought. It outlines the number of things (steps, items, processes, and so on) that needs to be completed during the performance of a task. This limits errors and accidents as well as increases consistency and accuracy.

The checklist is not a sophisticated piece of equipment that costs staggering amounts of dollars. It is probably the cheapest tool you could ever get. It is almost free! Just a piece of paper, yet it can and is saving lives, businesses, and careers.

Imagine the number of doctors and pilots that would be out of a job, serving jail terms (for negligence), or paying heavy fines if not for the power of this simple but effective tool.

One glaring example of the negative impact of not using a checklist especially during handling complex tasks is that of a two-year-old boy who was accidentally castrated by surgeons (The Guardian, 2019).

The boy who had an undescended testicle was scheduled for a routine operation that shouldn't take more than 30 minutes. However, after a grueling two-and-a-half-hour wait, his parents were informed that a camera had been mistakenly inserted into the wrong testicle and had damaged the healthy testicle. This meant that their son had been castrated. Of course, the hospital offered their sincerest apologies and also launched an investigation. This could have been avoided if the surgeons religiously followed the checklist.

While a doctor can offer his sincerest apologies for depending solely on his memory instead of a checklist, a pilot does not have that option. His life, crew members, and everyone aboard his airplane will be at a huge risk if he fails to use a checklist.

But is a checklist meant for only doctors and pilots? Certainly not! Nor is it limited to closing business deals or helping you to deliver a powerful presentation. Your checklist could be something as simple as your daily to-do list, grocery or shopping checklist, wedding checklist, packing checklist, moving checking, and so on. Depending on your memory to remember these details can slow you down, lead to mistakes – grievous ones – and appearing incompetent.

A checklist gives you a sense of accomplishment. As you cross things off your list, you get the inner satisfaction that you are making progress, and you'll naturally want to cross everything off. This increases your productivity level. It is also easier to delegate or enlist the help of another person when you have a checklist. The other person will know exactly what it is you want them to do since they are all written down. Additionally, a checklist helps you to be more organized knowing exactly what steps to take when performing a task.

Bottom Line: To make your tasks a lot less complicated, go over the things you do repeatedly at home or at work. Once you've identified them, create a checklist of all the steps required to perform that task. Now go ahead and begin to use that checklist. It will help you to minimize errors and increase the speed with which you complete your routine tasks.

Redundancy

How often have you heard the saying, "Don't put all your eggs in one basket?" Take the advice because it is good advice. Risking everything in a bid to secure a single venture doesn't really show thorough thinking and negates the second-order thinking. This is where the principle of redundancy comes in handy.

In Engineering, redundancy is the idea of including additional components into a system to checkmate system failure. It involves duplicating a system's critical components to increase the reliability of that system. In layman's terms, it is simply providing backups or backup systems that ensure the continuous functioning of a system even after a failure occurs.

For example, having more than one source of income in a family, including a spare tire in your car, backing up data in external hard drives, and so on. The main purpose of redundancy is to significantly reduce (or completely eliminate) any negative impact that can occur when a system fails.

How can you use redundancy in your daily life? And in what way does it improve productivity in your professional endeavor?

- Consider backing up critical information relating to your business not just on any hardware but using cloud programs. Also, create redundancy for critical parts of your business like getting a backup generator for your business (and home too).

- You can begin to think of ways to generate extra income or create an emergency fund just in case some unforeseen event happens and you lose your only source of income.

- If you are making an online presentation, for example, you could include both audio and text-only options for your users. The same goes for producing user manuals; you can include a paper manual alongside the audio version in case the audio doesn't work.

- If you are a business owner, you would understand that overdependence on an individual employee can result from specialization. To checkmate this, you can complement the principle of division of labor with the principle of redundancy. Here's how to do that. Identify the critical areas of your business – those areas that a single failure can result in the complete shutdown of your business. During your hiring process, enlist at least two people who can competently handle each of those critical areas. Of course, only one of them should man those areas while the other will handle other tasks. In the case where the employee handling the critical area is indisposed, you can fall back on your backup employee to temporarily handle the critical area.

Bottom Line: Take some time to think about the critical systems that exist in your life. Try to figure out what you would do if any of these systems fail and begin to put these backup plans in place. The earlier you begin to do that the lesser your chances of running aground would be in case of a system failure in your business or in your personal life.

Bottleneck (the Theory of Constraint)

The weakest link of a chain is the strongest point on that chain. If anything goes wrong with that weakest link, then it doesn't matter how strong the other links are; that chain is coming apart. This is the fundamental idea behind the theory of constraint or the bottleneck principle.

Every system – your physical body, your car, your company – has some constraints, but there is one constraint that is tighter than every other one. That constraint is called the bottleneck. The bottleneck is the point of greatest congestion that is capable of slowing down the entire system. It is similar to the weakest link on a chain – fix the bottleneck and the entire system will work better. Fix other constraints without first of all tackling the problem of the bottleneck, and it would just amount to a waste of effort as far as the entire system is concerned. For any improvement to affect the entire system, there is a need to first identify and remove the bottleneck.

Here is a simple example that shows how a bottleneck can slow down an otherwise efficient system. Let us assume it takes you under 15 minutes to drive to your place of work, but it takes another 45 minutes or more to find parking, it means that finding parking is a huge bottleneck in getting to work.

Buying a better car will be an effort in futility because it doesn't address the bottleneck.

Whether you are focused on personal development or concerned about improving your work, you must first understand that these things have different interconnected parts that make them all function as a whole. Your life may seem to you as if it is in shambles, and you are worried about fixing your life using different self-improvement programs. But not everything in your life needs fixing. If you do not identify your personal bottleneck, you will waste too much time and effort shouting into the wind. It may be that your bottleneck is your thinking process. Once that is fixed, every other part of your system will fall into place. In other words, more effort is not exactly what you need. What you need is to effectively apply the effort.

For example, if a task involving five steps takes about three hours to complete but more than two hours of that time is spent only on one of the steps, then shortening the time it takes to complete that one step will significantly improve the time it takes to complete the entire task.

Some of the common causes of bottlenecks in a work setting are:

- Waiting for information – especially if that information is critical to completing a task and the person to provide the information isn't forthcoming.

- Working in a team – this is especially true if one or more members are dragging feet on their part of the work.

- Perfectionism – as much as it is important to do a great job, constantly tweaking it to make it perfect can result in a huge waste of time.

- Handling unpleasant tasks – this is one of the causes of procrastination. You are likely to waste too much time getting started on a task that you don't enjoy doing.

- Difficult tasks – a task may not necessarily take much time to accomplish, but getting to understand how to handle it may take up too much time and effort. For example, putting in five hours of research time for a task that can be completed in 30 minutes like writing a dissertation on a topic you don't really understand.

To identify and eliminate bottlenecks, consider the following recommendations:

1. Try to figure out where you procrastinate. Most of the time, procrastination results from activities that are not mentally stimulating for you and can eventually lead to a bottleneck. You can remove this bottleneck by automating that task using software or apps. You can

also consider outsourcing such tasks.

2. Identify your creative blocks. Sometimes, we spend too much time on a task trying to figure out the best way to solve them. This can slow us down. You can eliminate this by splitting your creative tasks into two phases: idea-generation phase and idea-refining phase. Trying to accomplish both phases at the same time can lead to a creative block. First, gather as many raw ideas that are relevant to your task without bothering about tweaking them. After that, take the time to piece them together and refine them into a coherent whole.

3. When working in a group, what areas do you depend on others to complete your task? You may not have complete control over this, but you can speed up the process by taking precautionary measures to ensure that others are on the same page as you. Communicate early with team members. When you get a request to complete a task as a group, make sure to add extra hours (or days) to the deadline to take care of possible delays in the project completion.

Removing one bottleneck alone may not automatically fix every constraint in a system. However, it is the first step in allowing us to see other constraints in proper light. As you work on eliminating only one bottleneck at a time, your entire system gets better over time.

Bottom Line: Concentrate your effort on fixing your bottleneck first. Ignore every other so-called solution for other constraints. They don't impact the entire system. Remember that you can get your entire system working faster by fixing just one bottleneck.

Chapter 5: Getting Want You Want... Like This

In this final chapter, we are going to focus our attention on how to use mental models to improve our communication, particularly in the art of persuasion. You don't have to be a salesperson, a businessman, or a professional negotiator before you can effectively persuade others. There are quite a number of mental models that you can use to enhance your ability to think better during negotiations and persuading others, but we are going to consider only a few of them in this chapter. Before then, let us consider the common communication mistakes that people make in an attempt to persuade others to see their point of view.

Common Persuasion Mistakes

It is important to first distinguish between the different types of persuaders. Briefly, we all fall into one of these three categories:

1. **Detectives:** These are people who have a deep understanding of the art of persuasion. They employ the principles of persuasion and are honest in their attempts at creating a win-win situation for themselves and those whom they persuade. They don't rely on only one

communication approach for every person or people they encounter. Instead, they take their time to do the groundwork to get a good understanding of the mindset of their audience and then approach them accordingly. They do not come across as pushy and coercive in their persuasion even though they are assertive and know when to shift ground to allow mutual compromise. They don't set out to get the other person to agree to their position. Their mindset is always set on finding a middle ground that is beneficial to all involved.

2. **Smugglers:** These are people who understand what the correct principles persuasion are but prefer to cut corners by manipulating the other person or their audience. To the smugglers, following principles slows down the process of getting what they want, so they can lie, withhold critical information, exaggerate information, or distort the truth to get their way regardless of what their manipulation will cost others. Smugglers are those who are quick to twist the idea that the end justifies the means to suit their selfish agenda. They are not limited to corrupt politicians alone. Abusive spouses, manipulative bosses, dishonest salespersons, and many others fall into this category.

3. **Bunglers:** These are people who do not understand the principles of persuasion are, so they miss great opportunities to effectively communicate their point of

view. At every opportunity, they simply bungle their way through and fail to get the results they seek. Some of them may intuitively know one or two things about the techniques of persuasion, but they lack the skills to put them to effective use. They do not necessarily manipulate others like persuasive smugglers do, however, just don't know how to persuade people.

Now let us consider some mistakes that bunglers and smugglers make during persuasion.

Confusing Great Arguments for Persuasion

Presenting your point with sound reasoning and a lot of logic doesn't necessarily mean you will win the other person over. You need to make the other person see your position by connecting emotionally with them. As you know, emotions defy logic most of the time, so great arguments alone don't always work. Lacing your words with expressive and figurative language is necessary to tilt the odds in your favor.

Starting Out Too Strongly

Beginning with a strong stance is simply giving the other person a reason to object. Many people start out their persuasive process with a strong case and then try to push the other person over with a lot of enthusiasm and persistence.

This is almost always guaranteed to fail. Begin your persuasion without giving the other person something to fight against. Find a mutual ground and gradually nudge the other person towards your point of view or request.

Refusing to Compromise

Many people think that a compromise means surrendering their position. If you understand the principle of reciprocity, particularly the rejection-then-retreat technique you would know how to use compromise to your advantage. I'll explain how to use that technique in the next section of this chapter. When you refuse to shift ground, you are telling the other person that it is either your way or no other way. A compromise tells the other person that you are flexible and willing to listen to their concerns and viewpoints.

Thinking Persuasion Is a One-Off Event

Unless you are a persuasive smuggler who uses persuasion as a hit-and-run tool, persuasion cannot be used as a one-off event if you want it to yield a continuous effect. This is particularly true when you are trying to persuade a group such as your team, employees, entire family members, or an entire organization. Persuasion is a process that involves building credibility, stating positions, testing the positions, making compromises, and a continuous repeat of these processes until a mutually beneficial position is reached.

Assuming Your Message Is Understood

When you present your position without giving room for questions or input, you are assuming that your position has been accepted. If you have given a presentation, for example, give those who listened to your presentation the chance to ask questions no matter how powerfully logical your arguments are.

The Psychology of Persuasion

To increase our understanding of how to persuade others, let us take a quick look at Dr. Robert B. Cialdini's work on how social psychology intersects with marketing. His book, *Influence: The Psychology of Persuasion*, is widely considered one of the best works in the field of persuasion. The book focuses on six key principles that can be used to positively influence customers' behavior. However, we can apply these principles in our daily lives to help us improve our communication as it relates to persuading others. So, even if you are not trying to sell anyone any product or service, learning these principles can put you in an advantageous position. By the way, you can sell your idea and perspective to a loved one, friend, and colleague.

Persuasion Principle #1: Reciprocity

Imagine that your car won't start when you are already running late for work. Your neighbor gives you a ride to your office even their route is totally different from yours. You are grateful for their help, but you'll be on the lookout for a way to return the favor. Why? Reciprocity! It is an unwritten social rule that when you receive something good, it is expected that you reciprocate with a good gesture too. This is why we seem to behave nicer to those who are nice to us. Quantity or size doesn't matter in reciprocity; you may offer a total stranger an ordinary pen to write with when they need one, and in turn, they link you up with someone very influential.

Almost every business uses this principle to get potential customers to make purchases. It is no surprise to see free newsletters, ebooks, trial versions of products, webinars, reports, and so on target at offering prospects a taste of what they can get if and when they eventually make a purchase. Doing something nice for someone first puts them in the uncomfortable position of wanting to return the favor because if they don't, they'll feel shame on some level (whether real or perceived) and they'll be deemed ungrateful.

How does this apply to your daily life? To get others to be more receptive of you and increase your chances of persuading them, always be nice to them. The least they can do to return the favor is to listen to your proposition. It is easier to get someone to shift ground if they are morally indebted to you in some way. The key is to be the first to act positively towards them so that they "owe you one," and then you can call in the favor. This is applicable to people you know both on a professional and social level.

Persuasion is easier if the other person or people trust you. Sharing something important with someone is also another way to make them reciprocate by trusting you more. Be careful though not to give out information that others can use against you in the future.

Another way you can use the principle of reciprocity to persuade others is by asking for a favor that you know cannot be easily fulfilled. Then, when the favor cannot be met (an outcome you already envisioned), you make a second minor request which is what you originally wanted in the first place. Since your second request is significantly lesser than the first, it is easier and more likely to be fulfilled. This is known as the rejection-then-retreat technique. The idea behind this technique is that you are seen as willing to shift ground and come to a compromise even when it means sacrificing your first option. The other person will feel more inclined to reciprocate your compromise and sacrifice by fulfilling your request.

Keep in mind that the principle of reciprocity is intended to build trust that results in mutual benefits between people. This can only be true if you use this principle genuinely devoid of any agenda.

It is quite easy for those who do not understand the art of persuasion (bunglers) to confuse contracts with reciprocity. Feeling obligated to return a favor is very different than doing something based on some condition. A contract is generally in the form of I will do X on the condition that you do Y. Don't assume that someone who enters a contract with you is obligated to do you any favor or is open to considering your viewpoint. He or she is only bounded by the terms of the contract and not any social norm.

Persuasion Principle #2: Consistency and Commitment

Usually, we all want to appear to behave consistently with our commitments. Once we make a choice, especially an open one, we'll go to great lengths to maintain that image of ourselves. This means that if someone can get us to make a commitment, they can easily persuade us to do what appears consistent with that commitment even if that thing isn't really what we originally signed up for. The internal pressure we feel is usually linked to our desire to be seen in good light which is similar to seeking external approval.

The key to using this principle is to first get the other person to see themselves in a new (usually higher) light. Once you get their self-image in that new position, they are more likely to comply with a lot of your requests that help to maintain that self-image. For example, getting a customer to make their first purchase of something dubbed "exclusive" is a way to get them feeling that they belong to a higher income class. It would be easier to get them to make other expensive purchases since they would not want to be seen as inconsistent with their status.

You can use this principle to get others to agree to your requests especially if you can get them to make an open commitment or a written one. This can also work very well with getting colleagues in the workplace to behave in ways that are in keeping with their commitment. Asking a colleague what their goals and priorities are and then channeling your requests to conform with those goals and priorities will make it difficult for them to turn down your requests.

Another way to use this principle is to ask someone to do something instead of telling them. When you ask and get a yes, it increases the likelihood of the person doing what you want. Consider the following statements:

1. "Please, inform me on time if you can't keep the appointment."

2. "Will you please inform me on time if you can't keep

the appointment?"

The first statement simply tells a person what you want them to do and is less likely to make the other person keep the appointment. The second statement is a question, and it is framed in a way that engages consistency because the question appeals to their sense of commitment.

Do not try to use the principle of commitment and consistency to trick people into an agreement. Instead, see it as a tool to improve your chances of persuading others to agree to your genuine cause. In order to use this principle effectively, you must develop the ability to align your proposals and request with what others see as valuable. In other words, if your agenda is self-serving, it will be difficult to get others to see that your proposal will be beneficial to them. And even if you trick them into an agreement, as a persuasive smuggler would do, it will be difficult to keep up act unless you have the misguided understanding that a persuasion is a one-time event.

It is important to also know how to break yourself free from this way of thinking if someone is using this principle to make you agree to almost everything they want. First, you need to be sure of what your true values are and don't be carried away by approval-seeking behavior. If you feel internal pressure to behave consistently with some prior commitment which is no longer in keeping with your core values, do not hesitate to turn down a request. Don't be trapped by external social pressure and internal psychological pressure to do or agree to what you don't want to.

Persuasion Principle #3: Social Proof

Social proof, which can also be called herd mentality, is overdependence on what others around us are doing. Many times we look to how others behave to know if a thing is right or wrong especially in situations of uncertainty. If others are doing something, it is reasonable to consider it socially acceptable. After all, none of us want to be out of touch with the acceptable norm.

The need to fit in is our way of avoiding judgment. Marketing companies understand this, which is why they dub their products as the number one selling product! It makes sense for you to go for that product since the people buying can't all be wrong, right? Testimonials are also included in advertising where people who are just like you enjoy the benefits of product or service. All these are geared toward persuading you to do business with them.

How can you use social proof to persuade others in your life if you are not a sales representative or selling anything? First, understand that if you can show that a good number of people agree or accept your idea, it becomes easy to use that as social proof to persuade others. For example, instead of just telling someone to behave in a particular way, show them that all the other people in their group are already behaving that way. In other words, you are shifting their attention from the unwanted behavior (without necessarily judging it) to the wanted behavior by pointing out the positives of the wanted behavior. It works both at home and in the workplace because no one likes to be the odd one out, especially if what you are proposing doesn't contradict their core beliefs in a strong way.

A little caveat here – do not compel people to do want they truly don't want to do, especially if they are not violating any rule by being unique. Persuasion is not about getting every single person to agree with what you propose or to fulfill your request 100% of the time. Respect people's views and learn how to make compromises if that will make them shift ground. Persuasion reduces conflicts in your personal and professional relationships with others. If you are trying to persuade people and the conflict level in your relationships is on the rise, it shows you are not using the persuasion principles correctly.

Persuasion Principle #4: Liking

In ancient times, a messenger who brought bad news was killed! Why? It is for the same reason you like people who bring you pleasant news and tend to dislike people who are known to bring bad news even when they are not the cause of the bad news.

The principle of liking simply means that we like those who like us and are more inclined to listen to their suggestions or fulfill their requests. A salesperson who spend too much time describing how great his product or service is and all the benefits that customer can get from using his product or service may miss out on his opportunity to persuade the customer if they don't like him. Quite often, the difference between making a sale or not is whether the other person likes you. This is why a customer can bypass several stores selling an item he or she wants to buy just to get to a particular store because he or she likes the owner of that store.

Ignoring the principle of liking is throwing away a huge chance of connecting with your audience and making them pre-approve you. When people like you, they are predisposed to hear you out and receive your message.

Highlighting similarities increases your chances of being liked than emphasizing differences. This is where empathy and rapport building works magic. Giving compliments, especially genuine ones, can also help other people like you better. A compliment is akin to pleasant news, which makes the receiver likes the bringer of the pleasant news more. Many con artists have used compliments to distract their marks and get their way because we tend to be suckers for flattery, even if it is not genuine.

Taking the time to learn a few things about the person you want to persuade is a good way of connecting with them. You can't offer a genuine compliment about a person's positive traits if you don't know anything about them. Attempting that would give you away as a phony and ruin your chances of influencing them to do what you want.

Here's one other technique you can use to tilt people toward liking you more: improve your halo effect. The halo effect is a cognitive bias that makes us take one characteristic (or a few) and forms an opinion about a person, an organization, or a brand. Have you wondered why we tend to be shocked when a good-looking person behaves badly or a shabby-looking person turns out to be a successful millionaire? It is because we use one characteristic (in this case, their appearance) to judge their entire personality.

Marketing companies use the halo effect when they use a charismatic and attractive person in their marketing campaigns. Usually, they will get celebrities to use or wear their products. Since a lot of people like the celebrity, it stands to reason that they will also want to buy the product the celebrities endorse.

So, how can you improve your halo effect? Start by coming off as confident even if you don't have an attractive look in your own estimation. Don't neglect to work on your appearance (good nutrition, moderate exercise, and adequate sleep). Also, always put your best foot forward. It doesn't matter if you are meeting people face-to-face or through a medium like your website or blog, always think about the impression you want others to have about you and then channel your efforts towards making your personal brand reflect that image.

Persuasion Principle #5: Authority

This principle relates to our collective tendency to be easily persuaded by people in authority. You'll have certain reservations and may even out-rightly object if a person with the wrong credentials asks you to do a thing. However, if someone with the right credentials asks you to do the same thing, you are most likely to comply. For example, if a stranger tells you to take a certain drug for your ailment, you'll probably not listen to them. But if that same stranger is in a doctor's uniform with a stethoscope around his neck, you'll probably consider his advice. You may not heed his advice but the sign of his credentials (uniform and stethoscope) made you give him the benefit of the doubt.

This was how we were raised as children. Parents, teachers, and other adults rewarded us for obeying them and punish, scold, or show displeasure when we disobey them. So, we are conditioned to obey constituted authority. And by the way, that's a good thing – better than its polar opposite, anarchy.

When you try to persuade others, especially if the other person or your audience knows little to nothing about you, it is helpful if you say a few things about your credentials. Let them know why they should take you seriously. Be careful not to overdo it though as that can make you appear desperate.

Persuasion Principle #6: Scarcity

When the availability of an opportunity appears limited we tend to place more value on it. This is the basic idea behind the scarcity principle. The principle is somewhat similar to the loss-aversion mental model. The reason this principle works so well is that we tend to believe that things that are scarce are better than things we can easily acquire. We want something other people don't have or can't have because we want to be the ones who stand out.

"Limited copies available," "This offer is time sensitive," "This is the limited edition." Do you see how this works? Deadlines and limited availability are used to make something appear more valuable and makes it easier to persuade people to seize the opportunity. Advertisers use these types of lines to persuade people into taking action immediately because not acting immediately may mean they would have to wait and possibly miss out entirely. And no one wants to miss out.

The more your information or idea appears scarce, the more likely it is that you can persuade others to want to listen to you. Become less eager to get other people to see your point of view. Being readily available makes you appear desperate and too eager. Learn to keep your enthusiasm in check. Have you ever wondered why women play hard to get? Scarcity! The harder it is to get her attention (within reason), the higher the value a man places on her. Be assertive and confident about your position.

The Power of "Because": The Mental Model of Reason Respecting

One powerful way to get people to do what you want is to give them a reason to do it. When you tag your reason with the word "because," it can significantly increase the odds of getting others to comply with your request **because** it explains why they should. People usually resist change even without consciously realizing it. But when you give others a reason to do something different and highlight the reason with the word "because," it becomes easier to persuade them to do what you want. Consider the following statements used to encourage action from your website visitors:

1. "Call us now."
2. "Call us now because this offer is limited."

The first statement tells your website visitors what to do without a reason. The second statement tells them what to do and why they need to do it. You are giving them a reason (valid or not) to take action.

Take your mind back to when you were a little kid when your parents will tell you to do something like cleaning your room and you asked why. Even as a child, you resisted change. But when your parents would say, "because it's good to have a neat room", "because you're a good boy," or simply, "because I said so," you complied whether or not you understood the reason for their request.

We seem to need a justification to take action regardless of whether the justification is valid. The Copy Machine Study in the late '70s is a relevant example. Psychologist Ellen Langer headed a study in 1978 gathering data from a busy college campus photocopy center. Back in those days, Xerox machines were used for making copies and a lot of people waited in line to make copies in that photocopy center.

The study participants were given three different questions that were carefully worded to test people's response. They asked those waiting in line if they could skip the line and make copies. The following are the three questions and the responses as recorded in the study (Langer, 1978).

1. "Excuse me, I have 5 pages. May I use the Xerox machine?" Only 60% of the sample population said yes.
2. "Excuse me, I have 5 pages. May I use the Xerox machine because I have to make copies?" 93% said yes.

3. "Excuse me, I have 5 pages. May I use the Xerox machine because I'm in a rush?" 94% of the sample population said yes.

The first request had a low positive response because there was no reason given. The second and third request had very high positive responses because a reason was given. However, note that there was only a 1% difference between the second and third group of responses even though the third reason is more valid than the second. There was a 93% positive response without minding if the reason was bogus or not. "Because I have to make copies" is not a valid reason! Of course, you want to make copies! Why else would you be waiting in line in a photocopy center? This shows that we are somehow programmed to respond more favorably to reason than a bland request.

So, whether you are trying to get clients to agree to your proposal, get people to work with or for you, asking for favors from family and friends, or when you need just about anyone to do something for you, consider using the word "because" in your persuasion **because** you now know how powerful a tool it can be.

Warren Buffett: A Few Practical Lessons in Persuasion

The third richest man in the world (Forbes, 2019) and one of the most successful investors of all time, Warren Buffett is an incredibly persuasive individual. Psychologist Robert Cialdini explains why people easily pay attention to Mr. Buffet (and it isn't just because of his $79.4 billion net worth!)

In his book *Pre-Suasion: A Revolutionary Way to Influence and Persuade*, Robert Cialdini shows that great communicators (like Buffet and Munger) first prepare the minds of people to accept their message even without knowing what the message is. This is done through what Mr. Cialdini describes as pre-suasion: "The process of arranging for recipients to be receptive to a message before they encounter it" (Cialdini, 2016).

So, how does Warren use pre-suasion to persuade people? And most importantly, how can you use pre-suasion in your work and personal life? Here's how: first of all, establish credibility, disarm your audience, and then create a sense of unity. Here's how he demonstrates these steps.

Establish Credibility

There are several ways to establish credibility. One effective way Mr. Buffett uses is to show how believable and human he is. At every Berkshire Hathaway's annual shareholders meeting, Warren Buffett, alongside his partner, Charlie Munger, shares a short video that portrays them as honest and straightforward people. Usually, they make fun of the duo and humanize them. The goal of the video is to demystify their personalities and remove any notion that makes them look like know-it-alls and arrogant.

Also, during the questions and answers session, questions are allowed from not just the audience but also from financial journalists who have not been telegraphed beforehand. This is an open display of honesty and reinforces that in the minds of the audience.

The key lesson here is to come across as a relatable human who is ready to let his foibles show without feeling embarrassed or belittled by his humanity. In other words, making others feel that you can be accessible is a vital persuasion tactic. Equally, even if you have established prior believability, you need to make others see you as honest by being open about your processes. Keep in mind that persuasion is not the same as deception; therefore, your credibility must be seen as genuine.

Admit Mistakes

Many people would think that admitting your mistakes is

counterproductive as when you are trying to be effective at persuasion. But it isn't. Warren always admits his mistakes even in the presence of the shareholders of his company. In many instances, he begins his messages to audiences by admitting the mistakes his company had made in a previous year. For example, in his letter to shareholders in 2012, he began by saying, "for the ninth time in 48 years, Berkshire's percentage increase in book value was less than the S&P's percentage gain" (Stillman, 2017).

Admitting mistakes puts you in a good place to drive home your message because it first makes the other person or your audience to see the human side of you and also establishes you as a trustworthy source. You can prepare the minds of your audience to receive what you are about to persuade them about with this technique. Robert Cialdini explains that each time Mr. Buffett admits his mistakes, it opened him (Cialdini) up to be more receptive and to deeply process what Buffett had to say next.

Create a Sense of Unity

The idea you are trying to share with others or persuade them to accept is not as important as trust. If others don't trust you, they are not likely to accept your message and see things from your point of view. Buffett understands this and demonstrates it by making his audience feel they are part of his trusted group. Mr. Cialdini (2016) mentioned that he found Warren Buffett's 2015 message to shareholders of his company disarming. Mr. Buffett began his message by saying, "I will tell you what I would say to my family today if they asked me about Berkshire's future." This is a great way to gain the shareholders' trust. He gave the shareholders a sense of unity by using such personal connotations.

You can use this technique – making others feel they are part of your inner circle – to make people trust you more. The more other people feel they are part of your group or carried along on important issues, the more trust they have in you. A quick word of caution here: do not use this technique to trick people into trusting you. A truthful disclosure should be used as a smart means to earn trust instead of a shrewd way of getting people to believe what is untrue.

Conclusion

Your life does not get better than the quality of your thoughts, beliefs, and general perception. For any area of your life to improve, there is a need to adjust the thinking processes applied to that area.

We have seen how successful people do not rely only on hard work but also on smart thinking. Unconventional thinking or thinking out of the box is almost impossible if you do not open your mind to learning and accepting mental models. No matter how long and hard you work on coming up with a different decision or behavior using consensus thinking, you will simply be reinventing the wheel and at best, be making very insignificant incremental changes. Unconventional thinking may not be popular and may even be difficult and risky, but that's your best bet to making high-quality decisions that are capable of transforming your life, career, business, and relationships.

Knowing as many mental models as possible is a good thing; your ability to apply them to the various situations in your life is a different ball game entirely. I am not implying that you shun the quest for learning about different mental models. Instead, my emphasis is on knowing how to use them to solve your peculiar issues. Of what use is reading and accumulating knowledge if you cannot properly apply them in real life?

But the application equally requires a thorough understanding of the models. This means you need to be able to take a model and evaluate its usefulness in your situation before applying it. Applying a mental model to your situation because it worked for someone else, does not guarantee that you will record any form of success. You must first understand the nature of your situation and the combination of mental models you need to tackle the situation.

It doesn't matter the number of self-help books you read or the number of seminars you attend; you must develop the habit of thinking for yourself. Depending only on robotically applying the things you learn from books, seminars, and other sources, cannot handle the peculiar intricacies of your situation. That type of application has its limits of improvement. When you can take the lessons from the stories in this book, combine them with the principles explained, and then see how you can tailor them to meet your specific need – improvising where necessary, only then can you be said to have mastered how to use mental models to improve your life.

Your previously held assumptions can help ease the process of making routine decisions in both your personal life and professional endeavors. However, they can also constitute stumbling blocks upon which you constantly trip on your journey to a broader, better and more beneficial way of thinking. It can be a bit tricky to decide which of your previously held assumptions are beneficial or otherwise. Whatever you do, do not dismiss all your assumptions, concepts, and beliefs because you have found something new and better. Keep in mind that new truths tend to build on existing truths. Do a thorough mental house cleaning if you have to, but do not throw the baby out with the bathwater. I strongly recommend that you should take the time to carefully analyze how you came about your beliefs and determine if they are actually serving you or disempowering you and limiting your ability to think beyond their boundaries. A beneficial assumption or belief is not dogmatic; instead, it empowers you to think beyond your current state. It does not forbid you to reason beyond a certain point neither does it fetter you to consensus reasoning.

As you apply these and many more mental models you will eventually come across, keep an open mind about your definition of failure. If things don't work out the first time, it doesn't automatically mean you should throw the baby out with the bathwater! Perhaps Elon Musk has one of the most powerful quotes on failure. In his words, "There's a silly notion that failure's not an option at NASA. Failure is an option here. If things are not failing, you are not innovating enough" (Musk, n.d.).

Always have it at the back of your mind that the men you idolize in terms of success had (and still have) rough patches too. History is dotted with people who were considered failures during their trying moments but whom we now refer to as successful people. In 1985, Steve Jobs was considered a huge "public failure" when he was kicked out of Apple, a company he founded. Walt Disney was considered "not creative enough" and therefore fired from a newspaper. He later founded a film studio that soon went bankrupt. Steven Spielberg was considered unfit and was rejected twice from the film school at the University of Southern California.

These people didn't define failure as fatal. They understood that what they needed to do was to take a closer look at the thinking process that led to such failure and make the necessary adjustment. Thankfully, this book covers several methods you can use to correct flaws in your thinking process.

Here is one final caveat before I bring this book to a close: it is easy to drown in the sea of information. Do not spend too much of your time trying to figure out the exact mental model you need for every single situation in your life. Remember the advice of Jeff Bezos on prioritizing decisions. Not all decisions deserve the same amount of time and energy. If a decision can't be easily reversed, you will need to consider it very carefully. But spending all day considering every single decision you have to make very carefully means you won't ever get to decide on anything!

Sometimes you need to think on your feet. You cannot afford

to tell your boss, for example, that you need more time to come up with a yes or no answer to a minor decision (because you want to figure out which mental model to apply!) That will not put you in a good light and reduces your chances of getting any advancement in your career.

Don't allow the fear of deciding wrongly stop you from making any decisions at all. You are going to make mistakes! That is a given. Make peace with that fact and come to terms with learning from your mistakes. I did not write this book with the intention of making you completely avoid mistakes in your life. However, one thing is clear, the more you can put these time-tested principles to work in your life, the fewer wrong decisions you will make. The fewer mistakes you make during decision-making, the better your quality of life both on a personal and professional level.

It is my sincere wish that you would find the time to really study these mental models until they become second nature. That is only when you will reap the tremendous benefits of these mental models. And that also is when you can begin to think on your feet using this smart way of thinking.

Other Books by John Adams

1. **Masculine Emotional Intelligence:** *The 30-Day-EI-Mastery-Program for a Healthy Relationship with Yourself, Your Partner, Friends, and Colleagues.*

2. **Memory Improvement, Accelerated Learning and Brain Training:** *Learn How to Optimize and Improve Your Memory and Learning Capabilities for Top Results in University and at Work.*

References

Ahearn, B. (2014). *The 7 most common persuasion mistakes.* Retrieved August 20, 2019, from https://www.influencepeople.biz/2014/09/the-7-most-common-persuasion-mistakes.html

All Mind Tools (2018). *Rational decision making model.* Retrieved August 17, 2019, from https://allmindtools.com/rational-decision-making-model/

Andersen, R. (2014). *Elon Musk puts his case for a multi-planet civilization.* Retrieved August 20, 2019, from https://aeon.co/essays/elon-musk-puts-his-case-for-a-multi-planet-civilisation

BBC Worklife. (2014). *Why saying 'no' will boost your career.* Retrieved August 21, 2019 from https://www.bbc.com/worklife/article/20140314-just-say-no

Box, G. and Draper, N. (1987). *Empirical model-building and response surfaces.* Wiley; 1 edition (January 1987). ISBN-10: 0471810339

Brikman, Y. (2016). *A minimum viable product is not a product, it's a process.* Retrieved August 22, 2019, from https://blog.ycombinator.com/minimum-viable-product-process/

Bronner, S. J. (2012). *Campus traditions: Folklore from the old-time college to the modern mega-university*. University Press of Mississippi. ISBN 978-1-61703-617-0

BusinessDictionary.com. (n.d.) *Mental models*. Retrieved August 13, 2019, from http://www.businessdictionary.com/definition/mental-models.html

Cialdini, R. (2016). *Pre-suasion: A revolutionary way to influence and persuade*. Simon and Schuster, 1230 Avenue of the Americas, New York, NY 10020.

Clear, J. (n.d.). *All models are wrong: How to make decisions in an imperfect world*. Retrieved August 16, 2019, from https://jamesclear.com/all-models-are-wrong

Clear, J. (2019). *How to stop procrastinating and stick to good habits by using the "2-minute rule"*. Retrieved August 16, 2019, from https://www.lifehack.org/articles/productivity/how-stop-procrastinating-and-stick-good-habits-using-the-2-minute-rule.html

Clear, J. (n.d.) *Warren Buffett's "2 list" strategy: How to maximize your focus and master your priorities*. Retrieved August 22, 2019, from https://jamesclear.com/buffett-focus?source=post_page-----25c3724a5208----------------------

Cook, T. (2012). *Steve Jobs was an awesome flip-flopper, says Tim Cook (video)*. Retrieved August 20, 2019 from http://allthingsd.com/20120529/steve-jobs-was-an-awesome-flip-flopper-says-tim-cook/

Covey, S. (1989). *7 habits of highly effective people.* Simon and Schuster (2013 edition), 1230 Avenue of the Americas, New York, NY 10020.

Dalio, R. (2017). *Principles.* Simon and Schuster, 1230 Avenue of the Americas, New York, NY 10020.

DuBroff, R. (2017). *Confirmation bias, conflicts of interest and cholesterol guidance: Can we trust expert opinions?* Retrieved August 17, 2019, from https://academic.oup.com/qjmed/article-abstract/111/10/687/4587483?redirectedFrom=fulltext

Dyson, J. (2003). *Against the odds: An autobiography.* Texere; 2 Edition (April 17, 2003). ISBN-13: 978-1587991707

Elon Musk Quotes. (n.d.). *BrainyQuote.com.* Retrieved August 20, 2019, from https://www.brainyquote.com/quotes/elon_musk_750652

Encyclopedia Britannica, (n.d.). *Information theory: Physiology.* Retrieved August 16, 2019, from https://www.britannica.com/science/information-theory/Physiology

Faletto, J. (2017). *The Seinfeld strategy can help you be productive and prolific.* Retrieved August 16, 2019, from https://curiosity.com/topics/the-seinfeld-strategy-can-help-you-be-productive-and-prolific-curiosity/

Farnam Street (2019). *A lesson on elementary worldly wisdom as it relates to investment management & business.* Retrieved August 21, 2019, from https://fs.blog/a-lesson-on-worldly-wisdom/

Farnam Street (2018). *First principles: The building blocks of true knowledge.* Retrieved August 20, 2019, from https://fs.blog/2018/04/first-principles/

Farnam Street (2018). *The value of probabilistic thinking: Spies, crime, and lightning strikes.* Retrieved August 20, 2019, from https://fs.blog/2018/05/probabilistic-thinking/

Forbes (2017). *From Rockefeller to Ford, see Forbes' 1918 ranking of the richest people in America.* Retrieved August 22, 2019, from https://www.forbes.com/sites/chasewithorn/2017/09/19/the-first-forbes-list-see-who-the-richest-americans-were-in-1918/#4a81da3a4c0d

Forbes (2019). #303 James Dyson. Real time net worth. Retrieved August 22, 2019, from https://www.forbes.com/profile/james-dyson/#77d6022f2b38

Forbes (2019). Ray Dalio. Retrieved August 20, 2019, from https://www.forbes.com/profile/ray-dalio/#73bd1374663a

Grant, A. (2014). 8 ways to say no without hurting your image. Retrieved August 21, 2019, from https://www.linkedin.com/pulse/20140311110227-69244073-8-ways-to-say-no-without-hurting-your-image

Groopman, J. (2007). How doctors think. Houghton Mifflin Harcourt. ISBN 0618610030

Haden, J. (2019). Billionaire Jeff Bezos: People who are 'right a lot' make decisions differently than everyone else—here's how. Retrieved August 20, 2019, from https://www.cnbc.com/2019/03/12/amazon-billionaire-jeff-bezos-explains-why-the-smartest-people-change-their-minds-often.html

Hyatt, M. (2016). 5 reasons why you should take a nap every day. Retrieved August 21, 2019, from https://michaelhyatt.com/why-you-should-take-a-nap-every-day/

Indie Hacker (2018). Building a life-changing business with Austen Allred of Lambda school. Retrieved August 22, 2019, from https://www.indiehackers.com/podcast/046-austen-allred-of-lambda-school

Langer, Ellen & Blank, Arthur & Chanowitz, Benzion. (1978).

The mindlessness of ostensibly thoughtful action: The role of "placebic" information in interpersonal interaction. Journal of Personality and Social Psychology. 36. 635-642. 10.1037/0022-3514.36.6.635. Retrieved August 21, 2019 from https://www.researchgate.net/publication/232505985_The_mindlessness_of_ostensibly_thoughtful_action_The_role_of_placebic_information_in_interpersonal_interaction

McVagh, A. (2018). Mental model summary: Redundancy. Retrieved August 22, 2019, from https://www.mymentalmodels.info/mms-redundancy/

McVagh, A. (2018). Mental model summary: Social proof. Retrieved August 20, 2019, from https://www.mymentalmodels.info/mms-social-proof/

Melnyck, R. (2019). Second order thinking: This is how to make better decisions. Retrieved August 20, 2019, from https://primeyourpump.com/2019/03/04/second-order-thinking/

Munger, C. (2007). USC law commencement speech. Retrieved August 17, 2019, from https://genius.com/Charlie-munger-usc-law-commencement-speech-annotated

Munger, T. C. (2005). Poor Charlie's almanack: The wit and wisdom of Charles T Munger. Donning Co Pub; 2nd Expanded edition (December 30, 2005). ISBN-10: 157864366X

Poundstone, W. (2010). Priceless: The myth of fair value. Hill and Wang; First edition (January 5, 2010). SBN-13: 978-0809078813

Price, R. G. (2004). Division of labor, assembly line thought - the paradox of democratic capitalism. Retrieved August 22, 2019, from http://www.rationalrevolution.net/articles/division_of_labor.htm

Rampton, J. (2018). 6 common decision-making blunders that could kill your business. Retrieved August 20, 2019, from https://www.entrepreneur.com/article/313591

Scientific Thought: In Context. (2009). Physics: The Bohr model. Retrieved August 15, 2019, from https://www.encyclopedia.com/science/science-magazines/physics-bohr-model

Shapiro, J. (2018). Attorney general Shapiro announces $575 million 50-state settlement with Wells Fargo Bank for opening unauthorized accounts and charging consumers for unnecessary auto insurance, mortgage fees. Retrieved August 22, 2019, from https://www.attorneygeneral.gov/taking-action/press-releases/attorney-general-shapiro-announces-575-million-50-state-settlement-with-wells-fargo-bank-for-opening-unauthorized-accounts-and-charging-consumers-for-unnecessary-auto-insurance-mortgage-fees/

Shelley, A. (2019). 10 tips to KISS your life. Retrieved August 22, 2019, from https://www.lifehack.org/articles/communication/10-tips-kiss-your-life.html

Simmons, M. (2015). What self-made billionaire Charlie Munger does differently. Retrieved August 16, 2019, from https://www.inc.com/michael-simmons/what-self-made-billionaire-charlie-munger-does-differently.html

Sparks, C. (2017). 104: Systems thinking — The essential mental models needed for growth. *Understanding bottlenecks, leverage, and feedback loops.* Retrieved August 22, 2019, from https://medium.com/@SparksRemarks/systems-thinking-the-essential-mental-models-needed-for-growth-5d3e7f93b420

Stillman, J. (2017). *3 Killer persuasion techniques you can learn from billionaire Warren Buffett.* Retrieved August 20, 2019, from https://www.inc.com/jessica-stillman/3-killer-persuasion-techniques-you-can-learn-from-billionaire-warren-buffett.html

The Guardian (2019). *Operation on wrong testicle leaves two-year-old boy 'castrated'.* Retrieved August 22, 2019 from https://www.theguardian.com/society/2018/dec/21/operation-on-wrong-testicle-two-year-old-boy-bristol

Toth, P. P. (2015). *Treatment of dyslipidemia in elderly patients with coronary heart disease: There are miles to go before we sleep.* Retrieved August 17, 2019, from https://www.sciencedirect.com/science/article/pii/S0735109 715050032?via%3Dihub

Tracy, B. (2018). *The 80 20 rule explained.* Retrieved August 22, 2019, from https://www.briantracy.com/blog/personal-success/how-to-use-the-80-20-rule-pareto-principle/

Travis, C. and Aronson, E. (2007). *Mistakes were made (but not by me).* Houghton Mifflin Harcourt; 1 edition (May 7, 2007)

Wikipedia (n.d). *KISS principle.* Retrieved August 22, 2019, from https://en.wikipedia.org/wiki/KISS_principle#Origin

Wikipedia (n.d). *Thomas J. Watson.* Retrieved August 21, 2019, from https://en.wikipedia.org/wiki/Thomas_J._Watson